Education

ISSUES
(previously Issues for the Nineties)

Volume 35

Editor

Craig Donnellan

Educational Publishers
Cambridge

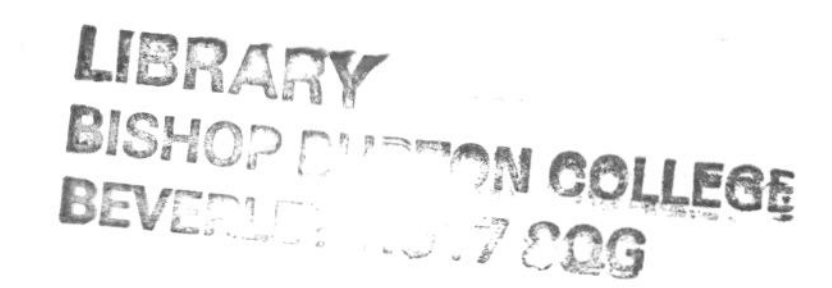

First published by Independence
PO Box 295
Cambridge CB1 3XP
England

British Library Cataloguing in Publication Data
Education – (Issues Series)
I. Donnellan, Craig II. Series
379.4'1

ISBN 1 86168 046 5

Printed in Great Britain
City Print Ltd
Milton Keynes

Typeset by
Claire Boyd

Cover
The illustration on the front cover is by
Andrew Smith.

CONTENTS

Chapter One: Declining Standards?

Chapter Two: The Cost of an Education

Introduction

Education is the thirty-fifth volume in the series: **Issues**. The aim of this series is to offer up-to-date information about important issues in our world.

Education looks at standards in education and the cost of further education.

The information comes from a wide variety of sources and includes:
Government reports and statistics
Newspaper reports and features
Magazine articles and surveys
Literature from lobby groups
and charitable organisations.

It is hoped that, as you read about the many aspects of the issues explored in this book, you will critically evaluate the information presented. It is important that you decide whether you are being presented with facts or opinions. Does the writer give a biased or an unbiased report? If an opinion is being expressed, do you agree with the writer?

Education offers a useful starting-point for those who need convenient access to information about the many issues involved. However, it is only a starting-point. At the back of the book is a list of organisations which you may want to contact for further information.

*****

UK lags on education

Britain has fallen from 35th place to 42nd in the world education league, according to figures from the Swiss-based International Institute for Management Development which David Blunkett, the education secretary, will present today to a teachers' protest rally in Hyde Park, London.

He intends to use a new batch of international statistics to demonstrate the failure of the previous Government's attempts to change the structure of schools instead of concentrating on improving standards.

'They have ignored the interests of parents, teachers and pupils, allowing class sizes to rise and they have failed to match our competitors so that we have fallen this year to 42nd in the world education league,' he said last night.

Tony Blair, the Prime Minister, has made frequent use over the last year of the Swiss institute's 1995 survey of business opinion in 48 of the world's largest economies to demonstrate the UK's lagging performance.

By John Carvel, Education Editor

Business leaders were asked how well their own country's education service met the needs of a competitive economy on a scale of 0 to 10.

In the 1996 survey, the UK scored less than three out of 10, slipping below China, Argentina and Turkey.

In the 1996 survey, the UK scored less than three out of 10, slipping below China, Argentina and Turkey

An international index of enrolment to higher education put the UK in 26th place, with 28 per cent of its young people aged 20 to 24 in universities and colleges, compared with 99 per cent in top-ranking Canada. The UK was 17th for public spending on education and 23rd for pupil-teacher ratios.

Thousands of teachers and school governors are expected to march through central London today to a rally organised by the National Union of Teachers to press the Chancellor, for a better deal for education as this year's public spending round comes to a conclusion.

Doug McAvoy, the union's general secretary, said the 4.5 per cent spending increase which the Government claimed to have delivered for schools this year was largely illusory.

A survey of 43 local authorities showed 10 cut spending per pupil this year and 20 set education budgets which failed to keep pace with inflation.

Others survived by raiding emergency balances, or cutting other services.

• *World Competitiveness Yearbook 1996*, IMD, Lausanne, Switzerland

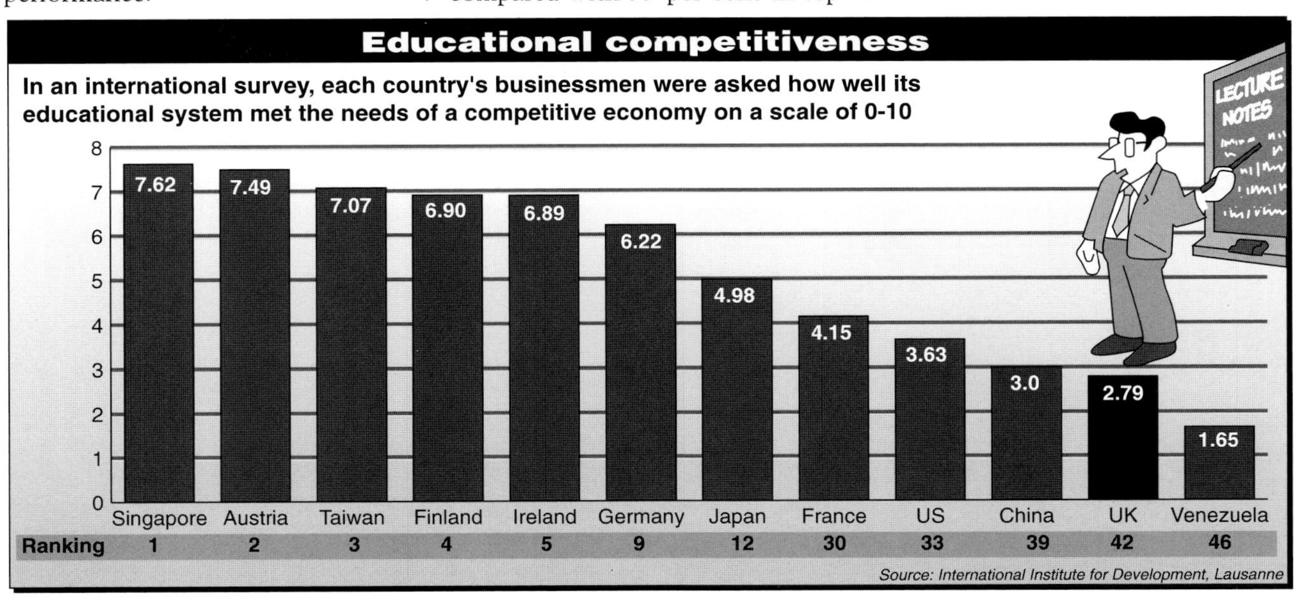

Why the English are bad at maths

By Lucy Ward, Education Correspondent

English nine-year-olds use calculators more and are taught less often as a whole class in maths lessons than children in countries which far outperform England in the subject, according to international research.

At secondary level, where England also lags well behind other nations in maths, 13-year-olds spend less time than their counterparts abroad on the subject overall and are set less homework.

A study published yesterday examines the influences which could explain the results of a major survey revealing that English children in both age groups struggle in maths compared with their contemporaries in Pacific Rim and other countries but outstrip them in science.

Its findings have already been seized on by David Blunkett, the Secretary of State for Education and Employment, as evidence to support the Government's drive for a minimum homework requirement.

In primary schools, children taught maths using traditional whole-class methods – the technique being advocated by the Government for literacy and numeracy teaching – were more likely to gain higher scores in tests set by researchers.

Meanwhile, countries – including England – where pupils routinely used calculators generally did worse in the maths league tables. England's relatively low ranking – tenth out of 17 nations – came despite the fact that primary schools spent more time on maths than virtually every other country in the survey.

However, the study found a very different picture in secondary schools. It revealed English schools were roughly in line with other nations on levels of whole-class teaching in maths lessons, but gave the subject less time than schools in other countries and set homework less often.

Thirteen-year-old pupils tended to do best in both maths and science in those countries where they had more lesson time and more homework, the research showed.

The findings are the second part of an international maths and science study, carried out in England by the National Foundation for Educational Research (NFER).

The first part looked at comparative performances of nine- and thirteen-year-olds in maths and science tests, while the latest section compares underlying factors such as time spent in lessons, class size, styles of teaching, levels of homework and teachers' and students' attitudes.

Researchers in England are particularly interested in the findings for the younger age group, because in primary schools children are taught both maths and science by the same teacher, yet achieve very different results relative to other countries.

Advocates of traditional teaching, including chief schools inspector Chris Woodhead, are likely to point to the study as evidence that whole-class teaching, mental arith-metic and plenty of homework are the crucial factors in achieving good maths results.

The same factors do not appear to have the same influence on science results.

However, Wendy Keys, one of three authors of the NFER report, stressed there might be no causal relationship between teaching styles and results. 'I don't want to say that you only have to use whole-class teaching and stop using calculators and you have solved it.

'Time spent and homework are the things to be looked at first before we start castigating teachers for not teaching the right way.'

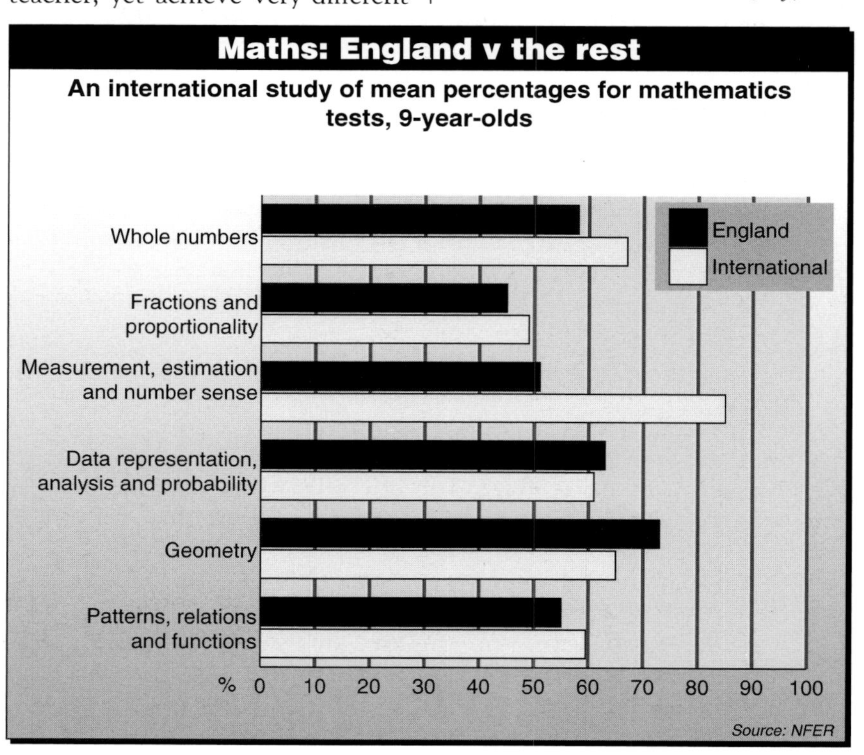

International numeracy survey

A comparison of the basic numeracy skills of adults 16-60 in seven countries

Most of the attention when the standard of performance in basic skills is discussed focuses on literacy. Partly this is because most of us have to read and (to some extent) write almost everyday. Yet increasingly evidence is becoming available about the importance of numeracy both in everyday life and in the world of work.

This small-scale International Numeracy Survey compares how well adults in seven countries, including the UK, handle some basic tasks involving numbers. The tasks included adding and subtracting decimals, calculating percentages and using fractions. They were all at a fairly basic level; for example 'What is 15% of 700?' and 'Subtract 1.78 from 5'.

The results for the UK are not very encouraging. People in the survey in this country answered fewer questions correctly than adults in any of the other countries – France, the Netherlands, Sweden, Japan, Australia and Denmark.

Of course, this was a small-scale survey and a larger survey, using different ques-tions, might have come up with a more encouraging result.

Whatever the current position is in schools, if this survey is right, we have been doing poorly in teaching numeracy for some time. Or perhaps other countries have recognised the need for good numeracy skills in the modern world rather more than we have.

• The above is an extract from the *International Numeracy Survey* by the Basic Skills Agency. See page 41 for address details.

The myth of educational golden days

By Judith Judd

If educational standards are falling, they have been falling for a very long time, an exam board suggested yesterday.

Tired of the annual round of complaints that GCSE and A-level exams are not what they were, the Associated Examining Board produced evidence that the cry of 'standards are falling' goes back for nearly 140 years.

The GCSE, say the critics, is a doddle compared with its predecessor, the O-level. Yet, the board points out, in 1985, during the golden days of O-level, four out of a group of 20 well-qualified trainee travel agents thought that Manchester was in Scotland.

One thought that Killarney was in Greece. On average, the group had six good O-levels each.

In the same year, British Midland Airways complained to the board that the most common error among its trainee reservation staff was that Bangkok was in Hong Kong and Brussels in Amsterdam.

Complaints by examiners and employers that young people cannot spell, punctuate or write grammatically are scarcely new.

In 1931, the Junior County Scholarship Examination Report listed 'tow' 'two', 'twelf', 'fivety', 'houndred' and 'severn' as commonly misspelt numbers.

'Spelling will always be a source of trouble in our language,' said the report. 'There was much confusion over such words as "steel" and "steal", "wring" and "ring", "alms" and "arms", "Wales" and "Whales", "rays" and "raise" . . . "It's" (the pronoun) was almost universally so spelt, though not greatly to the surprise of those who constantly receive letters subscribed "Your's sincerely".'

And if schools are blamed today for not teaching grammar, the critics are following in a long tradition. In 1858, examiners protested that the 'the principles of Grammar as exhibited in the English Language are not made a matter of systematic study in our schools'.

The examining board's director responsible for liaising with industry, George Turnbull, said: 'Almost 140 years later we hear the same comment from those who should know better. It's time they stopped making a drama where there is no crisis – other than the one that has always been with us.

'These examples illustrate that it was ever thus, and though we should always strive to improve, the euphoric glow of past grandeur and excellence in education must remain a figment of a fertile imagination.'

Officials admit: it is easier to pass exams

By Liz Lightfoot, Education Correspondent

The Department for Education has admitted for the first time that the steep rise in the number of pupils passing exams at top grades is partly due to easier papers.

After years of denying that standards had slipped, the department acknowledged yesterday that both A-level and GCSE had suffered from 'grade inflation'.

The volte-face came after a speech by Prof. Michael Barber, head of the Government's School Effectiveness Unit, in which he said that improved results were partly due to good teaching, but the picture was not straightforward.

'In part, there has been an element of grade inflation. That seems to be a view shared by the experts,' he told a conference in London. When the GCSE replaced O-level in 1988 there had been 'teaching to the test'.

He added: 'That is something that happens whenever you introduce a new exam system. Grade inflation has probably been brought to an end now, but it has happened.

'It is not the sole cause of the rise in the pass rate, but it has been a factor. It has historically played a part.'

Successive Conservative education ministers had refused to accept that more were passing exams because they were easier and accused those querying the increase of devaluing the achievements of pupils and teachers. Only last month education ministers rejected the charge after another rise in exam passes.

Yesterday, however, a spokesman for the department said: 'There may have been a degree of grade inflation in the early years of the GCSE.' She said that A-levels had also been affected. However, she said that as a result of measures taken by the School Curriculum and Assessment Authority to tighten up procedures 'we believe this has now been eliminated'.

Those querying standards have included employers who reported lower levels of literacy and numeracy among job applicants despite their good exam passes. Universities, too, complained that A-levels had become easier and that undergraduates no longer had the solid grounding in their subjects that they used to have.

The rise in exam successes masked low standards in some schools, particularly in numeracy and literacy.

The GCSE was introduced 10 years ago to replace O-levels and the CSE examinations taken by less academic pupils.

The top three A-C grades are supposed to equate to the same three O-level grades and CSE grade 1, and originally grades D and E were meant to equate to both lower O-level and higher CSE grades.

The numbers gaining the top three grades have risen from 39.8 per cent of the entry in 1987, the last year of O-level, to 54.4 per cent this year, and the proportion awarded an A or *A has doubled over the same period to 14 per cent. The proportion of candidates awarded the top two A-level grades is now 30 per cent higher than in 1989.

The exam boards, however, maintained that standards had not fallen. George Turnbull, of the Associated Examining Board, challenged Prof. Barber to produce the experts who believed there had been grade inflation.

'I don't know how he can make statements like that without the evidence which all goes the other way.' A report by Her Majesty's Inspectors on the first two years of GCSE had concluded that the new exam had been a success, he said.

Last year, a Government inquiry into exam standards over time concluded that courses had changed radically, but found no conclusive evidence that standards had slipped.

Exams that create an underclass

By John Carvel, Education Editor

Head teachers warned last night that the Government's 'obsession' with the results of the most able GCSE candidates was contributing to the growth of an underclass of school drop-outs.

As the exam boards for England, Wales and Northern Ireland reported another slight increase in the proportion of candidates getting good grades, attention was focusing on the chronic failure to lift the bottom end of the range.

David Hart, general secretary of the National Association of Head Teachers, welcomed a 0.4 per cent increase in numbers of GCSE passes at grades A to C – equivalent to the old O level. The proportion of papers passed at good grades has increased every year since the GCSE was introduced in 1986 and now stands at 54.4 per cent.

But Mr Hart said the Government was making a huge mistake in its plan, disclosed in the *Guardian* yesterday, to put even greater emphasis on the upper grades by setting a national target to raise the proportion of 16-year-olds getting at least five.

'It is patently ridiculous that the achievements of those who do not achieve a C grade or better are inadequately recognised,' Mr Hart said. David Blunkett, the Education and Employment Secretary, was 'replicating the attitude of the previous administration', which encouraged parents to judge schools by league tables showing how many pupils got five good GCSE passes.

'This year's results demonstrate that the perpetual emphasis on A to C grades is damaging the interests of the less able.' There was a slight reduction in numbers achieving the lower grades and no improvement in the overall pass rate. About 50,000 pupils leave school each year with no GCSE passes at all.

Teachers were being encouraged by the league tables to concentrate on pupils who could get the good grades. The tables should be converted to a points system – similar to A levels – which could recognise achievement at every level of ability.

The proportion of papers passed at good grades has increased every year since the GCSE was introduced in 1986

'The Government's obsession with the more able candidates is damaging the least able, thereby contributing to the growth of the underclass, the socially excluded whom Labour is now urgently seeking to rescue,' he said.

Mr Blunkett is preparing targets

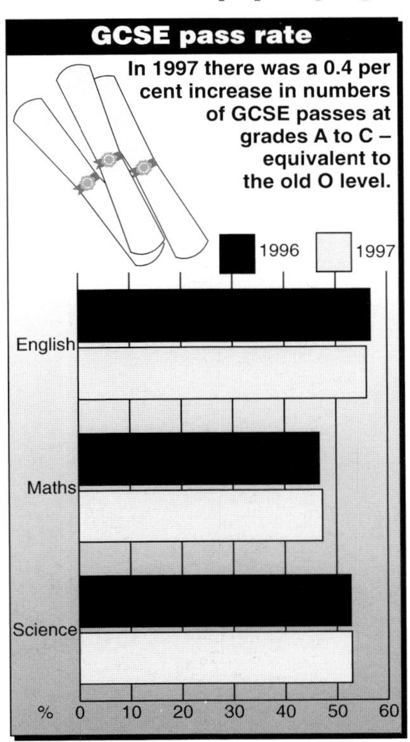

to achieve a leap in the number of 16-year-olds getting grade C or above in at least five subjects. A national target to be set in the autumn will be converted for local education authorities and schools.

But his officials disputed Mr Hart's claim that the plan would encourage teachers to forget the low achievers. The targets would help the Government deliver its goal of producing a skilled workforce with at least 85 per cent of 19-year-olds with good GCSEs or equivalent vocational qualifications. Other measures, including better vocational courses and youth training, would tackle the problem of pupils leaving without any passes.

Kim Howells, the junior education and employment minister, said the improvement in higher grade pass rates was a 'tribute to the hard work of the candidates and the dedication of their teachers'.

He was concerned, however, about a drop of nearly 1 per cent in the proportion of candidates getting good grades in English. There was also a 2 per cent fall in numbers taking the subject.

The results provoked another round of the seasonal debate over whether improvements rate were due to a better performances or devaluation of exam standards.

Roger Young, director general of the Institute of Management, said 57 per cent of managers thought GCSE standards had dropped over the past 10 years.

But Denis Lawson, chairman of the joint council of GCSE exam boards, said it took its responsibility for maintaining standards seriously. Doug McAvoy, general secretary of the National Union of Teachers, said critics of the exam had failed to make their case.

Results reveal big gulf in standards

By Cherry Norton and Julian Guyer

Kent, Lincolnshire and Berkshire have been revealed as the local education authorities with the best performing schools in Britain for A-levels.

Schools from the three counties make up almost a fifth of the top 300 secondaries, which have been ranked according to the proportion of their A-level entries resulting in A or B grades. By contrast, a third of the 140 education authorities in England and Wales, including Cornwall, Suffolk and Humberside, failed to get any schools in the top 300.

Educationists say the stark differences in performance are not solely explained by the number of academically selective grammar schools in successful areas or the social background of their pupils, but also reflect wide variations in standards across the country.

Kent has 29 schools in the top 300, headed by Tonbridge Grammar School for Girls, which comes 14th. It is followed by Lincolnshire, with 13 in the top 300, and Berkshire, with 12. By contrast, Cambridgeshire and Hampshire have no schools in the top 100.

Top of the 'first division' of 100 schools is Chelmsford County High School for Girls, which had 72% of its A-level entries graded at A or B. Of the top 100, 70 are grammar schools. Half are grant-maintained schools which have opted out of local authority control but face losing their status under government plans to increase councils' powers over them.

However, 28 comprehensives reached the top 100 despite not selecting pupils according to academic ability. The highest performer is Queen Elizabeth's Boys' School in Barnet, which came second to Chelmsford. It is followed by Watford Grammar, and Dame Alice Owen in Potters Bar. All three are grant-maintained.

The biggest risers overall among grammar and comprehensive schools are mixed and under local authority control. Lady Lumley's, a mixed comprehensive in Pickering, North Yorkshire, recorded the biggest improvement, rising from 288th to 74th place.

Sir Thomas Rich's School in Gloucester was the highest riser among the grammar schools. It moved from 251st to 47th place. Ian Kellie, the headteacher, said: 'I think that one thing in our favour is that we only offer traditional A-level courses and subjects – we have no modular exams, just those which have academic credibility with the universities.'

Single-sex schools continued to dominate the upper ranks of the table, with only four mixed schools appearing in the top 20; two of these are boys' schools which have girls in the sixth form. This lends support to claims by some educationists that pupils achieve better results in a single-sex environment.

Girls are still outperforming boys – 35 of the top 100 were girls' schools, compared with 20 boys-only schools.

School standards conflict

Donald MacLeod reports on differences of opinion over a delayed report

The inquiry set up by the Government to settle the argument over A-level and GCSE standards failed yesterday to come to a clear conclusion and left the main protagonists in continuing conflict.

Wrangling between Chris Woodhead, head of the Office for Standards in Education, and Nick Tate, head of the School Curriculum and Assessment Authority, delayed the report's publication, and yesterday the two men were putting different glosses on the report.

Mr Tate insisted there was evidence to show falling standards over the past decade, while Mr Woodhead said nothing had been proved and there was a danger of children being taught for longer and longer and learning less and less.

Exam results have risen dramatically both in grades and the proportion of children taking A-levels and GCSEs, but employers and university academics in subjects like maths have complained about the knowledge and skills of young people they see.

At 16-plus, 43.5 per cent of pupils obtained five C grades or better last year compared with only 22.6 per cent in 1975, in what was O-level. At 18-plus, the percentage obtaining two or more A-level passes rose from about 12 to more than 20. England is not alone; the proportion obtaining the French baccalaureat has doubled to 50 per cent since 1975 and the percentage gaining the abitur in Germany rose from 10.7 in 1970 to 26.9 in 1991. What is unique is the increased proportion of candidates passing.

Boys trail behind girls as pupils improve in tests

By Liz Lightfoot, Education Correspondent

Pupils improved their performance on national curriculum tests this year but the results published yesterday showed a worrying gap between boys and girls.

For the first time, more than 60 per cent of 11-year-olds reached the level expected for their age in English and maths and 69 per cent in science. At 14, the pupils improved their scores in maths and science compared with last year but did slightly worse in English.

Figures for the tests taken by 1.8 million children, however, highlighted the under-performance of boys which the Government must tackle if it is to reach its targets of 80 per cent of 11-year-olds reaching the standard expected in English by 2002 and 75 per cent in maths.

Boys who, according to data by local authorities, are less articulate when they start school, lag significantly behind girls by the age of seven. Ten per cent fewer seven-year-old boys than girls reached the expected level in reading, writing and spelling. By the age of 11, the gap had grown to 12 per cent fewer for English and at 14 it had widened to 19 per cent.

However the same boys could hold their own in maths. Girls, who started with a three per cent lead at seven, lost it to boys at 11 when two per cent more boys reached the required standard. By 14, results were equal. Girls did slightly better at science aged 11 but fell by two per cent at 14.

John Coe, of the National Association for Primary Education, said boys were not catching up with girls by the time they reached secondary school.

'We need to focus particularly on boys between four and seven because English is the key to the rest of the curriculum.'

Under-achievement by boys was also a problem for society. 'We need to look at the influence of fathers because, though mothers are responsible for most early language teaching, boys see their fathers as role models and are likely to be influenced by their attitudes to such things as reading.'

Estelle Morris, Schools Standards Minister, said results confirmed that 'our ambitious literacy and numeracy targets are achievable'.

Another concern, she said, was spelling where only 62 per cent of seven-year-olds reached their expected level.

Results for seven-year-olds showed 80 per cent reaching the required level for reading and writing compared with 78 and 79 per cent last year. In maths, 84 per cent hit the target compared with 83 per cent last year.

By the time they reached 11, 63 per cent had reached the expected level in English, 62 per cent in maths and 69 per cent in science, compared with 58 per cent, 54 per cent and 62 per cent last year.

At 14, 55 per cent reached their level for English and 60 per cent for maths and science compared with 57 per cent for all subjects last year.

English pupils might be no good at maths but they are world-beaters at solving practical maths and science problems, according to a survey published yesterday.

Findings from the recent third International Maths and Science Study placed English children tenth out of 17 countries in maths but fifth in science. Those results related to performance in written, knowledge-based tests.

Another part of the study looked at children's performance in practical tests, using science and maths skills.

They were asked, for example, to construct a scale model of the interior of a house, with items of furniture, and calculate from their measurements which could be moved from one room to another.

Girls and boys reaching required standards

	Boys	Girls	Both (this year)	Both (last year)
Age 7 % reaching required standard				
English (reading)	75	84	80	78
English (writing)	75	85	80	79
English (spelling)	56	68	62	n/a
Maths	84	82	84	83
Science	84	86	85	84
Age 11 % reaching required standard				
English	57	69	63	58
Maths	63	61	62	54
Science	68	69	69	62
Age 14 % reaching required standard				
English	66	47	56	57
Maths	60	60	60	57
Science	61	59	60	57

Source: Ofsted

Girls beat the language trap

One in three children still starts secondary school behind in the three Rs, new test results show.

Although National Curriculum test scores have markedly improved, a third of all 11-year-olds still lack the reading, writing and arithmetic skills expected of their age group – a gap they may never be able to close.

And boys are lagging behind girls in English. At seven, three-quarters of boys are hitting the target, but by the time they start their GCSEs, less than half can read, write and spell at the expected level.

Girls are slightly behind in maths at all stages while the sexes are equal on science.

But the results for seven, 11 and 14-year-olds, published yesterday, showed improvement at all ages. Teachers and the Government welcomed the scores.

Since the tests were taken in the spring, Labour has set new tougher targets as part of a campaign to boost children's numeracy and literacy by 2002.

By Gaby Hinsliff, Political Reporter

School standards minister Estelle Morris hinted at changes for next year's tests. She said: 'We shall continue our work to ensure we tackle head on the under-achievement of boys in English.'

At seven, three-quarters of boys are hitting the target, but by the time they start their GCSEs, less than half can read, write and spell at the expected level

The Government has announced a package of measures to raise standards; including training teachers to teach the three Rs, summer schools for struggling pupils, and setting aside daily 'hours' for literacy and numeracy in primary school.

Education watchdogs Ofsted suggested yesterday that tests in maths may need to be made harder in order to stretch children.

Teaching unions said the results testified to teachers' hard work despite constant criticism.

Doug McAvoy, general secretary of the NUT, said: 'It is hard to square this solid evidence of improvement with some of the more apocalyptic announcements coming from Ofsted.

'It is now time for cool analysis of the conditions which help create success rather than falling back on blanket criticism of teaching and teachers.'

Schools are now likely to meet Government targets which require 80 per cent of 11-year-olds to be at level four in English and 75 per cent in maths by 2002.

League tables for primary schools will also be published shortly.

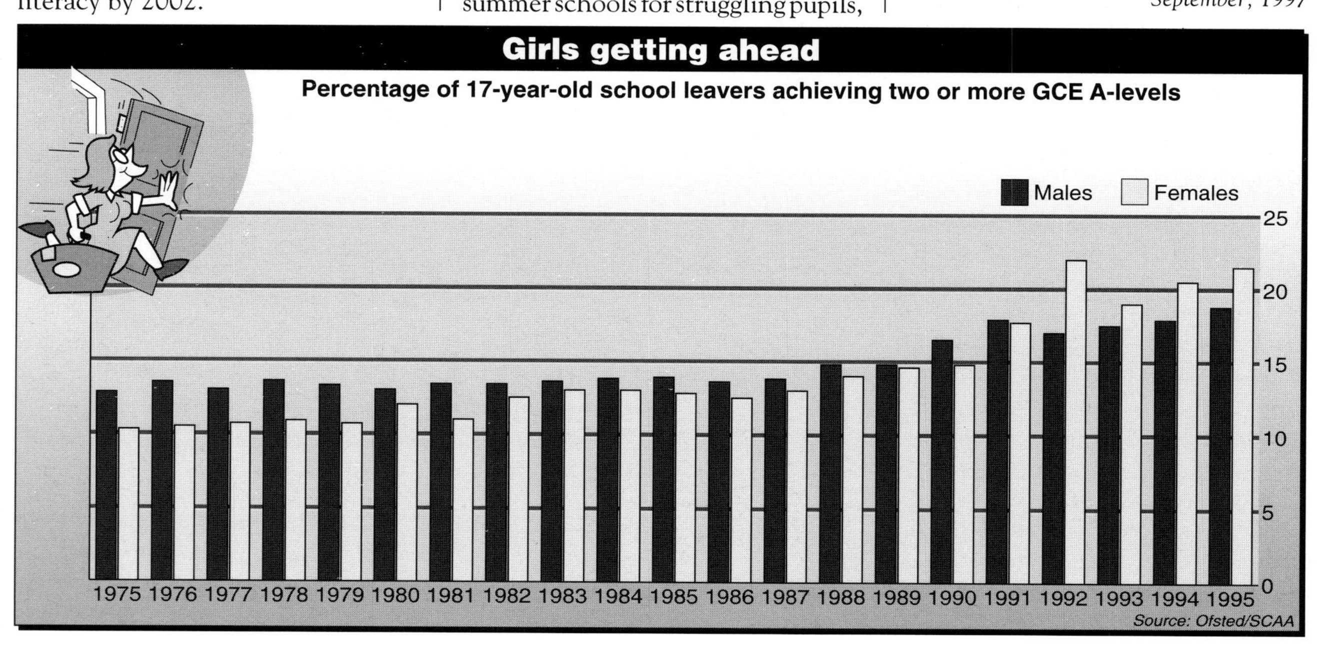

Top examiner says 'easy grade' system is undermining A-levels

By Judith O'Reilly, Education Correspondent

One of Britain's most senior A-level examiners has warned that claims of rising standards are being undermined by fundamental failings in the examination system.

David Burghes, chairman of examiners for mathematics with one A-level board, says standards are being compromised by unchallenging syllabuses and papers which make it easier for pupils to get certain grades.

Burghes, professor of mathematics education at Exeter University, says the result is that the big increase in the A-level pass rate in England and Wales from 70% in 1985 to 87% this year might not reflect a real improvement in standards. He compares it with Scotland, where the pass rate in Scottish Highers, the A-level equivalent, has risen by only 3% in the same period.

'Our standards and expectations in numeracy and literacy are unacceptably low and although this new government is taking steps to improve the situation, setting targets and improved exam success is not necessarily the same as real improvement,' says Burghes.

The comments from such a senior figure within the examination system will intensify the debate about standards. Ministers are considering changes to A-levels to make them broader, possibly by increasing the number of subjects students take.

In an article in *The Sunday Times* today, Burghes identifies one of the key problems as being the number of commercial examination boards offering A-levels and GCSEs, which enables schools to shop around for what they perceive to be the easiest.

'A perceived "easier" award undoubtedly attracts more candidates – and more income for the board – in future years. We all know this, but there is a conspiracy of silence,' he says.

'The increase [in the pass rate] has become substantial and it is perhaps unfortunate that we have more than one exam board, as it is tempting to conclude that grade inflation is at least in part due to competition between boards.'

Burghes criticises GCSE examinations which use tiers of papers, where it is easier to get certain grades on one set of tiered papers than another. So, for example, on an intermediate tier, pupils can attain only grades B to E, while on a higher tier they can get grades A to C.

'Our research has shown that both the B and C grades can be obtained more easily on the intermediate tier; candidates must achieve higher marks but on a much more restricted syllabus than in the higher tier,' says Burghes.

Jim Brennan, an A-level classics examiner for the past decade and a classics teacher for 40 years, agrees that standards had fallen. Candidates taking classical civilisation A-level were unable to differentiate between 'there' and 'their', 'would of' and 'would have' and regularly misspelt words such as 'allowed' as 'aloud'.

Vivian Anthony, former chief examiner of economics A-level and now secretary of the Headmasters' Conference, which represents independent schools, said: 'Generally, answers are getting better but where I think there has been more concern expressed is at the bottom end and some of those who now scrape through with E grades would not have scraped through 10 years ago.'

Examination board officials maintain that A-levels, GCSEs and marking regimes are regulated by the School Curriculum and Assessment Authority. They say examinations are rigorously marked and the awards are an accurate reflection of candidates' abilities.

Inspectors sent to the bottom of the class

By Judith Judd, Education Editor

School inspectors, who spend their days telling teachers that they could do better, are themselves given poor marks in an unpublished report seen by *The Independent.*

The report, from the Office for Standards in Education, the inspections watchdog which awarded the same inspectors their contracts, says their reports are vague and woolly, and use sloppy grammar and punctuation.

Chris Woodhead, the Chief Inspector of Schools, has said repeatedly that reports must be well-written so that they can be understood by schools and parents. A review by Ofsted, which looked at 400 reports completed during the summer and autumn terms last year, says that the writing of one in seven school inspection reports is not up to scratch and few are good throughout. One in seven has very good features.

Grammatical errors occur in many: the most common is the lack of agreement between a verb and its subject.

The apostrophe, downfall of many pupils, also catches out the inspectors, for example: *Childrens'*. 'Punctuation is generally accurate but there are reports in which the use of the apostrophe is erratic, with omission, misplacement and even superabundance.' They are accused of bad grammar: 'Attainment and progress is good'; truisms: 'When teaching is good, pupils are challenged': jargon: 'Continuity and progression'; vagueness: 'Teaching is usually satisfactory or better.'

Inspectors are accused of inconsistency. Reports tend to start off by painting 'an unduly rosy picture of a school' but then they change their tune.

One in seven school inspection reports is not up to scratch and few are good throughout

One begins by noting that 'teaching promotes sound educational standards' yet the same report reveals that progress in one-third of lessons is not up to standard and pupils are underachieving in many subjects.

In many reports, judgements are vague. 'Skills in spelling and writing are less well developed.' Less well developed than what?, asks the watchdog's report. And what do terms such as 'some', 'variable', 'uneven' or 'mixed' mean when they are used without explanation?

Doug McAvoy, general secretary of the National Union of Teachers, said that the inconsistency between and across reports had been one of teachers' concerns. 'Ofsted must put in place quality control for its own inspection judgements.'

Parents to get schools 'hotline'

By Rebecca Smithers, Education Correspondent

The Government is planning a telephone hotline for parents to lodge complaints about schools, a move condemned by teachers last night as 'unacceptable interference' and 'policy on the hoof'.

Education and Employment Secretary David Blunkett revealed the plan at a London conference where he was launching a national consultation exercise on raising school standards that will shape the future of education in Britain.

He said he had asked his department to provide a 'helpline' where parents could get advice on a wide range of education and school issues.

But teachers complained that the hotline – which will be policed by the department's School Standards and Effectiveness unit – would encourage parents to make irresponsible complaints when well-established procedures were already in place.

David Hart, general secretary of the National Association of Head Teachers, said last night that he was appalled at the suggestion that the Government was encouraging parents to phone into the department if they did not get satisfaction from schools.

'This smacks of Big Brother and is a form of completely unacceptable interference in the way that schools are run. Only last week the Prime Minister was saying that the role of head teachers should be strengthened. This is clearly policy on the hoof which has been ill thoughtout.'

A spokesman for the department, however, strongly denied that the proposal was designed to undermine head teachers, and insisted that it was an attempt further to involve parents, who were already at the heart of the consultation exercise.

'The advice line would guide them towards other agencies who might be able to answer their questions. The advice line is not an attempt to undermine head teachers or schools.'

Mr Blunkett said he did not intend the helpline to be something parents could use to 'whinge' about their schools.

'We would hope and expect teachers to support the idea,' said the spokesman.

Mr Hart added: 'It is not the job of central government to interfere in this way and I think the teaching profession will be deeply worried by it.'

Schools show progress as more pupils make grade

This year's national test results for 7-, 11- and 14-year-olds, published yesterday, show some progress towards government targets for the year 2002. But this year's improvement is smaller than last year's and there is still a long way to go. Judith Judd, Education Editor, looks at the latest figures.

For the first time, more than 60 per cent of 11-year-olds have reached the expected standard or better in both English and maths.

Ministers have set targets for 80 per cent achieving the required level in English and 75 per cent in maths. Estelle Morris, the schools minister, said that this year's results showed that the targets were achievable.

If the improvement continues at this year's rate, the targets will easily be met by 2002. However, the biggest rise in achievement usually occurs in the first years of a new test or exam as pupils and teachers become accustomed to it.

Ms Morris said the Government could take credit for the higher results because of its standards campaign before and after the election. 'These results show our continuing highlighting of the importance of literacy and numeracy – and primary school homework – is clearly having an effect in the classroom.'

But she said that there was still much work to do to achieve the targets.

Pupils are awarded one of eight levels in the tests. For seven-year-olds, the expected level is two, for 11-year-olds four and for 14-year-olds five.

The most worrying results are those for 14-year-olds. After remaining much the same for two years, the proportion reaching the required standard or better was up slightly in maths and science at 60 per cent.

In English, it was down from 57 per cent reaching the expected level to 56 per cent.

For 11-year-olds, the improvement in maths (up 8 per cent) is greater than that in English (up 5 per cent). Last year, the figures for both subjects were up 10 per cent. Science results, which have always been better than those in the other two subjects, are up from 62 per cent to 69 per cent.

Girls continue to outstrip boys in English but in maths, the boys were just ahead. Overall, 16 per cent did better than the expected level in English and 18 per cent in maths.

At age 14, 6 per cent were above the required standard in English and 11 per cent in maths. Only 1 per cent were at the top level (eight) and less than half a per cent did even better than that and showed 'exceptional performance'.

Seven-year-olds did slightly better than last year with around four-fifths reaching the expected level in English and 84 per cent in maths. But only 62 per cent achieved the required standard in spelling tests which were compulsory for the first time this year.

Nigel de Gruchy, general secretary of the National Association of Schoolmasters/ Union of Women Teachers, said: 'I congratulate teachers and their pupils on these results and hope that the Government will amend its advice to the pay review body in the light of this improvement in productivity.'

Better literacy may not benefit the economy

Universities are groaning at the seams, but think tank says poverty relief rather than better education is the key to prosperity

By Judith Judd, Education Editor

Ministers should end child poverty instead of spending more on education if they want to raise school standards, according to a new report.

Tony Blair's slogan 'education, education, education' is mistaken, says Peter Robinson, author of the study from the Centre for Economic Performance, an independent research unit at the London School of Economics.

This direct challenge to the Government's belief that better education leads to a stronger economy comes the day after the Prime Minister, Tony Blair, underlined the Government's pledge to raise standards in schools with an education summit.

The Downing Street event brought ministers and civil servants together with 40 headteachers and others from the education world to discuss themes which included boosting school leadership, stretching children of average ability, improving teaching quality and tackling under-performance.

The report argues against these approaches. 'A serious programme to tackle child poverty might do far more for boosting attainment in literacy and numeracy than any modest interventions in schooling.'

A study of comparative performance in international maths surveys over the last 35 years shows that the scores bear very little relationship to economic performance. While the growing Asian economies do well, so do the Slovak Republic and Bulgaria.

'The two most successful small Asian economies, Singapore and Hong Kong, had in 1985 adult literacy rates of 14 and 12 per cent.' The rate in advanced industrial economies is less than 1 per cent.

The report followed people born in the same week in 1958 and 1970 and suggests that class size, homework, setting and streaming and teaching methods have no impact on literacy and numeracy, but social class does.

'The two most successful small Asian economies, Singapore and Hong Kong, had in 1985 adult literacy rates of 14 and 12 per cent'

The only impact schools can make is shown in the finding that working-class children learn more if they are educated with middle-class children. Mr Robinson said the findings suggested that children did best in socially mixed comprehensives.

The report points out that, though the economy does not benefit from higher literacy and numeracy standards, individuals do. Yet the Government's present policy of targets ensures that schools have little incentive to concentrate on the bottom 10 or 15 per cent of pupils.

At GCSE that meant that the least able were neglected because the Government target was five A-C grades (the three top grades).

In primary schools, the target was for all pupils to reach Level 4 in maths and English, suggesting that teachers should concentrate on those who are just below average. Level 3 for all would be a better target because it would compel teachers to pay more attention to the least able, Mr Robinson said.

He added: 'The Government says that at the moment we have an education system that benefits the few and not the majority. It is the other way round. The system benefits the majority but not the few at the bottom.'

Poverty row looms over literacy drive

By Rebecca Smithers, Education Correspondent

The Government will today tell the worst performing education authorities that poverty is no excuse for failure, as it details tough reading targets all their primary schools must meet.

The School Standards Minister Stephen Byers will also tell a London conference that the worst performing authorities must double their pupils' reading standards.

The new literacy targets are designed to meet the Government's key aim that by 2002, 80 per cent of children should be reading at the required standard for their age as they start secondary school.

The poorest performing authorities will be told that a minimum of 70 per cent of their 11-year-olds must be up to this standard within four years. The Government will monitor schools' performance and those wide of the mark will be 'named and shamed', and may have a government 'hit squad' sent in.

Some inner-London boroughs – including Hackney, Tower Hamlets and Newham – now have fewer than 40 per cent of 11-year-olds reading at the required standard. But under the new guidelines even better performing authorities – such as Richmond, which is achieving almost 80 per cent – will be told to aim for 90 per cent.

Although the targets are in theory subject to negotiation with local education authorities, officials yesterday said there would be little scope for change. Teachers' unions will be furious at the extra burden placed on them, and the authorities will be angry at the Government's insistence on drawing attention to schools at the bottom of the league.

Mr Byers will, however, try and soften the blow by making it clear that the poor performing authorities will be able to apply for cash from the Government's standards fund to help them set up new literacy programmes and other initiatives. The minister will also court controversy when he tells conference delegates that inner-city poverty will no longer be an excuse for failure. He will point out that some schools with more than half the children eligible for free school meals are already on course to meet the targets.

Eamonn O'Kane, deputy general secretary of the career teachers' organisation NASUWT, said: 'We worry about the additional bureaucracy of more detailed targets and what that will mean for our members' growing workload. We also believe that poverty has to be recognised as a factor in teaching, as children from seriously deprived homes are often at a disadvantage in the classroom.'

On Wednesday, the Government will publish a review of the framework for children with Special Educational Needs. A green paper will set out proposals to get parents more involved in decisions for their children and to cut out many of the bureaucratic assessments.

Older and younger

The basic skills of different age groups

Whether standards have declined in recent years cannot be answered conclusively by our survey. The number of people assessed was relatively small and not all basic skills were measured. Moreover, factors such as nerves, lack of familiarity and sight and hearing defects have to be taken into account in drawing conclusions from the result of a single assessment.

It's clear, however, that older people did much worse than younger people on average and that competence with basic skills tends to decrease as people pass middle age. Of course, it's not true of everyone and some older people did extremely well in the survey. Surprisingly, women appear to do worse than men, not just with basic maths but in reading. All previous evidence has suggested that women are rather better than men at reading and writing, but slightly poorer when using numbers. Of course, much previous research was based on self-report and our survey indicates that this is a fairly unreliable way of judging basic skills competence. A larger survey concerned with gender differences (and making sure that tasks didn't favour men or women) is needed to be certain about the differences in performance between women and men.

What is clear is that too many people have fairly limited basic skills. These tasks were not, in the main, that difficult yet a significant number of people couldn't cope with them. We have long been concerned with raising standards in respect of these crucial basic skills. Our survey suggests that we can ill afford to put off this urgent task.

• The above is an extract from a summary of the publication *Older and Younger – The basic skills of different age groups* produced by the Basic Skills Agency. See page 41 for address details.

Basic skills projects get £32m boost

More than £32 million raised by the National Lottery is today ploughed into improving basic literacy and numeracy of children and adults.

The lottery charities board admits it is tackling 'real educational need'. But it denies breaching the principle that lottery money should not substitute for state funding.

Janet Paraskeva, the board's director for England, said: 'Of course this is a need which should be met by the main educational programme, but unfortunately it has not been so for a little while now.'

The cash represents a quarter of a £126 million grants programme announced today. The £32 million will go to 356 charities and community groups working to improve numeracy and literacy.

Last week, a government report said more than 8 million people of working age have such poor literacy that they cannot complete forms or work out sums.

Many of today's grants will go to groups working with ethnic minorities. Ms Paraskeva cited one scheme, the Claudia Jones Organisation in Hackney, east London, which is receiving £227,000 over three years for its after-school and Saturday classes for Afro-Caribbean pupils.

'It is an excellent project and a perfect example of where mainstream education is not doing as well as it should for this particular group,' Ms Paraskeva said.

By the board's own admission, the grant programme echoes some central themes in the Government's white paper on reforming the lottery. Ministers plan to take £1 billion a year from lottery receipts for a 'new opportunities' cause to benefit education and health.

The board insists that it decided two years ago to fund literacy and numeracy schemes and that its intentions have been endorsed by wide consultation.

By David Brindle, Social Services Correspondent

More than 8 million people of working age have such poor literacy that they cannot complete forms or work out sums

The biggest grant today is £632,000, for development of a new community centre in a former mining area at Riccall, near Selby in North Yorkshire. Riccall Regen 2000, the group receiving the money, was set up last year.

A total £628,000 is going to the Salterbeck Alliance for Community enterprise in Workington, Cumbria, to provide training, employment and volunteering opportunities in a purpose-built resource and sports centre.

Kids' Club Network, which promotes out-of-school child care throughout the country, is receiving £455,000 towards its work which is central to the Government's ambitions for getting lone mothers off benefit and into work.

Anne Longfield, the network's director, said the cash was 'a significant boost', but did not replace the need for government investment to help more clubs start up.

The Child Bereavement Trust, which trains professionals in how to deal with families who suffer the loss of a child, is awarded £107,000. Jenni Thomas, who founded the trust, was last year highly commended in the Guardian Jerwood charity awards.

One in five adults on bottom rung of literacy

By John Carvel, Education Editor

More than 8 million Britons of working age have such low literacy that they cannot fill in forms or work out sums, according to a survey published yesterday by the Office for National Statistics.

About 22 per cent of Britons aged 16-65 performed at the bottom level of an international test of ability to comprehend written information. Of seven other countries in the survey, only Poland had a higher proportion of under-performers.

However, Britain also had 17 per cent of the five-band scale, beating Switzerland, Germany and the Netherlands, but behind the United States, Canada and Sweden. Those in the top bands could cope with specialised language, dense texts, subtle inferences, complex displays of information, and streams of sums.

David Blunkett, the Education and Employment Secretary, said the results showed 'there has been an unacceptable neglect of literacy standards for too long . . . Nothing less than a drive to make us a nation of lifelong learners is needed if we are to improve our place in an ever more competitive world.'

The statistics office said the survey, the first using a national random sample of 3,800 working-age adults, comprised 45 tasks based on 15 documents to assess three types of literacy: prose literacy (ability to understand newspapers and passages of fiction), document literacy (ability to use timetables, graphs, charts and forms), and quantitative literacy (ability to solve maths problems by picking out numbers found in texts).

For all three, the proportion of Britons at the lowest level of performance was higher among the over-45s. But there was little difference between the age groups 16-25, 26-35 and 36-45, suggesting there had been little change in educational attainment among school-leavers over the last few decades.

About 22 per cent of Britons aged 16-65 performed at the bottom level of an international test of ability to comprehend written information

Those with lower levels of education were more likely to be at the lower literacy levels, but researchers found graduates at the bottom level as well as people who had top-level skills after having left school early. There was no difference between literacy in England and Scotland, but Wales had fewer reaching the highest level of prose literacy – 9 per cent, compared with 17 per cent in England.

Working adults and full-time students were more likely to perform at the top levels on all three scales. The unemployed were twice as likely to show the lowest level.

Alan Wells, director of the Basic Skills Agency which sponsored the survey, said it showed the problem was worse than had been thought. 'It suggests we have a greater number of people with weak reading skills than almost all of the other industrialised countries in the survey.'

He said there should be a campaign to improve adult literacy. 'Without it we will write off generations who cannot benefit now from more effective teaching in schools.'

Mr Blunkett promised a white paper on lifelong learning before the end of the year. The Government's literacy task force is due to publish its final report next week, proposing a daily literacy hour for all primary pupils, summer schools, and remedial courses for 18 to 24-year-olds lacking basic skills.

Poor marks

Among the 8.4 million Britons propping up the international literacy scale:

- 46 per cent need help when filling out forms;
- 30 per cent need help to write a letter;
- 13 per cent need help reading instructions on medicine bottles;
- 73 per cent say they are satisfied with their reading and writing skills;
- 60 per cent think their reading skills are good or excellent;
- 10 per cent think their reading skills are poor.

Source: *Adult Literacy in Britain*, Stationery Office, £30.

Where it all goes wrong

John O'Leary analyses an international study of primary school teaching

Seldom can a piece of research have confirmed as many theories as this week's third International Mathematics and Science Study. It made depressing reading, in maths at least, but next month's analysis of the possible factors behind the results should be even more revealing.

The study, the largest and most reliable of its kind, showed nine-year-olds in Scotland and England languishing in the bottom third for maths of the 26 countries taking part. Like last November's tests of 13-year-olds, the research confirmed a long-suspected weakness in basic numbers work.

Only in geometry did English pupils top the table. In calculations involving whole numbers, English children registered fewer than 60 per cent correct answers, while those in Singapore managed almost 90 per cent.

The tables were turned in the science tests, where the extra time that English schools give the subject and its comparatively late introduction in some countries may have conferred an advantage. Most experts consider the maths results a more accurate benchmark of achievement.

What, then, accounts for Britain's slide down the international league table? Changes in the countries being assessed make it impossible to gauge the steepness of the decline. Nevertheless, the US, Canada and Ireland have all overtaken England since the last survey, in 1991.

Comparisons of teaching methods to be published in next month's report will strengthen the Government's hand in demanding changes in primary teaching. The leading countries are using more whole-class teaching, setting more homework and using calculators less than in England or Scotland.

The jury is out on the effect of class size; countries such as Hungary and Canada, which have smaller classes than England, do achieve better results. But top-rated Singapore has 11 pupils more per class on average and Japan has four more.

Nor is there a straightforward relationship between the amount of time spent on maths and national success in the tests. While Singaporean pupils spend about an hour a week more on the subject than their counterparts in England and Scotland, the Japanese, with nearly two hours' less teaching, do almost as well.

The correlation is much stronger with traditionalist hobby-horses such as the use of calculators, whole-class teaching and the amount of homework given to pupils. England and (even more so) Scotland are totally out of line with the countries used in the detailed comparisons on the proportion of time spent teaching the whole class.

Even the United States and the Netherlands devote five times more attention to this method of classroom organisation. Despite this, the penchant of British teachers for group work means that the proportion of time spent on individual tuition is lower than in Holland and the US.

The contrast is just as striking in the use of calculators. Effectively denied to nine-year-olds in Singapore and Japan, they were used more than once a week in more than half of the schools in England.

In the setting of homework, too, Britain is out of line with almost all the other nations, the exception being the Netherlands, where most nine-year-olds are not expected to work out of school. The proportion

How different countries teach maths

	Singapore	Japan	Netherlands	Hungary	US	Canada	Scotland	England	Norway
Lesson time hours/week	5.5	3.7	4.7	3.3	4.2	4.4	4.3	4.6	3.0
Average class size	39	32	24	22	24	24	26	28	19
Homework set at least once/week %	98	89	15	99	94	75	59	47	100
Teacher teaches whole class most/every lesson %	68	78	60	53	54	37	3	11	64
Pupils use calculators once a week or more %	1	1	4	14	39	29	–	53	1
Children who believe they do well in maths %	77	74	85	84	91	94	90	90	91

Source: Third International Mathematics and Science Society

of English pupils set homework at least once a week is half that in Singapore, Hungary and America.

Government advisers will consider that the findings vindicate many of their recent initiatives, especially as most of the issues are common to all subjects. Calculator-free tests have already been introduced. Labour promised homework guidelines for primary schools before the election and the new Literacy Taskforce is certain to base its recommendations on greater use of whole-class teaching.

A Fabian Society seminar held in London this week suggested that there will be no let-up in the requirement for more traditional teaching methods. Though the Government was conscious of the need to raise morale in the teaching profession and keen in theory to give staff more scope to make their own decisions, improving results was the priority. Central direction would be used where particular strategies were shown to work successfully.

Here lies one of the dilemmas facing ministers: their stated aim of combining 'pressure and support' for schools is hard to put across successfully when different audiences have to be addressed.

Tuesday's much-trailed proposal for a 'literacy hour' in primary schools, for example, was intended to give schools an opportunity to shape a much-needed initiative. By the time the small print of the announcement could be examined, however, the move had been portrayed as a crude response to failure.

British pupils lead world in computer access

By John Carvel, Education Editor

British schoolchildren have more access to computers than their counterparts in any other country, according to a survey published yesterday.

As education ministers prepare an information technology strategy to link all schools with the Internet and improve teacher training in computer skills, the study showed Britain at the top of the league for computer literacy among pupils.

'Britain has proportionately more schools with computers than any other nation, and more pupils have access to them. Britain has also gone further down the road in introducing information technology in schools, with spending on computers and information technology in secondary schools up tenfold since 1985,' said the report by Italian-based Olivetti Personal Computers.

Britain is the only country to have at least one computer in every primary school, compared with 97 per cent in the US, 94 per cent in Canada, 91 per cent in France, 70 per cent in Japan and less than 10 per cent in Germany.

Primary schools have on average 10 computers each and a ratio of one for every 18 pupils, compared with one per 500 pupils in Germany.

Secondary schools had on average 85 computers each – one for every 8.5 pupils – double the provision in Germany and even further ahead of Japan, France and Italy.

'More than £1 billion has been spent on introducing IT into the nation's schools since 1979 to put Britain into a world-beating position,' the report said.

There was also a dramatic increase in computer ownership in households with children. A representative survey of more than 2,000 pupils found 66 per cent used a computer at home, compared with 45 per cent two years ago. In almost 20 per cent of households with children, there were at least two computers. One in five computer-owning households was connected to the Internet.

On average, a child with a home computer spent about 11 hours a week using it – an increase of 10 per cent on last year. Most children under 11 thought computers could help them learn, but only a third of children in their early teens shared this view.

Literacy of Britons lagging far behind industrial rivals

By Liz Lightfoot, Education Correspondent

Britain has come third from bottom in a league table of literacy covering eight industrialised countries, according to a survey published yesterday.

People in Britain are less able to follow a recipe, use loan interest charts or work out sale bargains than those in most of the other countries surveyed.

Though the Office for National Statistics, which analysed the data, gives warning of the difficulty of comparing the eight countries, the pattern of low achievement in Britain across the ages of the participants and the tasks they performed is inescapable.

It showed that more than one in five adults in the country have very poor literacy standards. About 8.4 million Britons of working age (22 per cent) are incapable of comparing and contrasting two pieces of information.

Poland contained the highest numbers of illiterate or semi-illiterate young people between the ages of 16 and 25, followed by the United States, Britain, Canada, French-speaking Switzerland, Netherlands, German-speaking Switzerland, Germany and Sweden.

Only four per cent of the age group in Sweden had difficulty understanding written information, three per cent could not read charts and five per cent were unable to do exercises such as working out savings from sale advertisements. In Britain, the proportion was far higher at 17, 18, and 22 per cent.

Results for the next age group, 26-35, were similar. Eighteen per cent of Britons could not understand prose in newspapers or information booklets, 19 per cent could not read charts and 20 per cent had difficulty working out bargains in shops and supermarkets. In Germany the numbers in each category were 12, six and five per cent.

The study on a random sample of 3,800 people in Britain, who carried out 45 tasks on 15 documents, was largely funded by the Department for Education. David Blunkett, the Education Secretary, said the survey confirmed his fears about the quality of literacy skills.

'It shows that while we perform well in some skills there has been an unacceptable neglect of literacy standards for too long which the new government is now addressing head-on,' he said.

'Sound literacy and numeracy skills provide the bedrock for all subsequent learning. We have appointed an advisory group on adult learning, and we will soon be publishing a policy paper on life-long learning.'

Across the age ranges, those over 45 were more likely to have worse literacy standards than the younger groups but there was little difference between those aged 16-45.

There was no difference between literacy standards in England and Scotland, but Wales had fewer adults reaching the highest level.

Alan Wells, director of the Basic Skills Agency, which helped sponsor the study, said it showed the problem was worse than previously feared. 'It suggests we have a greater number of people with weak reading skills than almost all of the other countries in the survey.'

Despite their poor showing, Britons were generally confident about their abilities. Though more than half – 52 per cent – were on the lowest of five levels for interpreting textual information the study found that 86 per cent described their skills as either 'excellent' or 'good'. Only 11-16 per cent thought their reading, writing or mathematics skills were limiting their job opportunities.

Basic Skills Programmes for Adults 1994-95

We received information from 638 organisations managing literacy and numeracy programmes and 488 organisations managing ESOL programmes. We believe that this represents almost all of the provisions being made in England and Wales

People receiving help with literacy and numeracy – 1994-95 Academic Year

The figures for this year are not directly comparable with figures for previous years. Previously statistics focused on a 'snap-shot' in one week and this did not give an overall picture of the scale of basic skills provision for adults. In future years we intend to concentrate on cumulative totals.

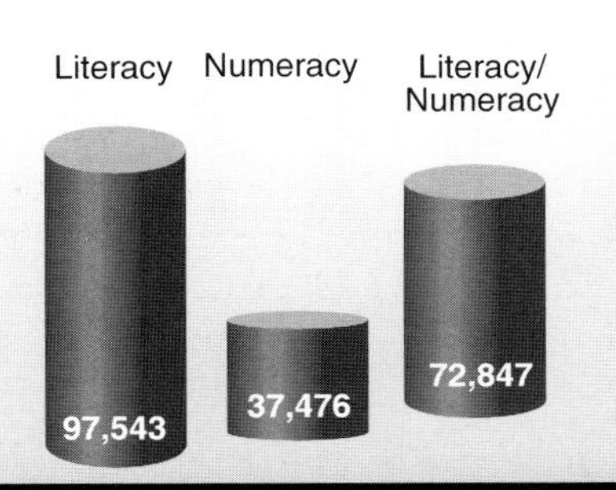

	Literacy	Numeracy	Literacy/Numeracy	Total	ESOL	**Total**
England	93,886	35,832	69,693	199,411	98,959	**298,370**
Wales	3,657	1,644	3,154	8,455	451	**8,906**
Total	97,543	37,476	72,847	207,866	99,410	**307,276**

123 abc 456 xyz 789

Providers

Colleges are now the major providers of basic skills; more than half of the people in basic skills programmes are in further education colleges. A decade ago LEA adult and community education services would have been in the position colleges are in today. The number of people receiving help with ESOL in prisons is overstated because of returns from one contractor for 11 prisons. These prisons have a large throughput of people on remand or detained on entry to the UK. Many receive minimal instruction.

	Lit/Num England %	ESOL England %	Lit/Num Wales %	ESOL Wales %
FE Colleges	62	52	63	68
LEAs	21	22	30	23
Training Organisations	4	*	7	9
Voluntary Organisations	1	*	–	–
Prisons	10	23	–	–
Other	2	3	–	–

* = less than 1%

Literacy and Numeracy provision in England

FE Colleges 62%
LEAs 21%
Prisons 10%
Training Organisations 4%
Other 2%
Voluntary Organisations 1%

Source: Reaching Out, Annual Report 1995/96, The Basic Skills Agency

Pupils sink in world maths league

By Donald MacLeod, Education Correspondent

Children in primary schools in England are falling further behind children in other countries in mathematics but are among the best at science, the largest ever international education study reported yesterday.

Teachers in England and Scotland set less maths homework and do far less whole-class teaching than in the Pacific Rim countries, which topped the league of 26 countries, according to the Third International Mathematics and Science Study of the performance of nine-year-olds. More than half of the English children used calculators compared to only 1 per cent in Singapore and Japan.

Yesterday's study confirms the disturbing picture of deteriorating maths performance among 13-year-olds published last year. England and Scotland were behind Hong Kong and other Pacific Rim countries, the United States, Canada and Australia, and other European countries, including Ireland, Hungary, the Czech Republic and Slovenia.

But in science, English children were behind only Japan, Korea and the United States. This reflected the increased time devoted to science and training for teachers since the introduction of the national curriculum, said Wendy Keys, co-author of the report.

Maths standards could be affected by a range of factors including rising class sizes, teacher morale, the amount of homework, and use of calculators. Nine out of ten English and Scottish nine-year-olds thought they did well in maths, compared to 74 per cent in Japan and 77 per cent in Singapore. 'Teachers have fostered a positive self-image but we have to ask whether teachers are accepting lower standards than they should.'

The study, involving 175,000 nine-year-olds in 4,000 schools in 26 countries, asked questions in six areas of maths. English children performed below the international average except in geometry and data handling.

The study confirms the disturbing picture of deteriorating maths performance among 13-year-olds published last year

Overall English pupils got 57 per cent of the answers correct (Scotland 58 per cent) compared to 76 per cent in Singapore, 74 per cent in Japan and 63 per cent in the United States.

Just over half the English children correctly turned 4+4+4+4+4=20 into a 'multiplication fact' (5x4=20), compared to an international average of 76 per cent and 94 per cent in top-scoring Singapore.

'Improved' results in maths are challenged

By Liz Lightfoot, Education Correspondent

Billions of pounds spent on the national curriculum have failed to raise maths standards in primary schools, according to a study published today.

It claims that the 18 per cent rise in the number of 11-year-olds reaching the required standard for maths over the last three years is because of changes in tests, not improved performance.

The research, by Manchester University, published in the *Times Educational Supplement* today, involved 1,500 children in five Manchester schools. It found there was no significant improvement in the performance of either seven or 11-year-olds in the eight years since the national curriculum was introduced.

Julie Davies, who carried out the study using a maths test provided by the National Foundation for Educational Research, blamed overloading of the primary curriculum for reducing the amount of time teachers could spend on maths and literacy.

'Our measure has stayed the same over the last eight years whereas the national tests have changed,' she said.

'The national curriculum was introduced in 1988 to raise standards but it is clear from the tests we have carried out in literacy and in maths that it has failed to improve performance in the basics.

'Primary teachers all know the importance of teaching the basics but tell us they have been squeezed out by all the other subjects they have to teach, such as history and geography and science.

'If we are right then billions of pounds have been wasted and national tests do not do the job they are supposed to do.' According to national test figures, the number of 11-year-olds reaching the standards expected for their age has gone up from 44 per cent in 1995 to 54 per cent last year and 62 per cent this year.

The standardised maths scores of 11-year-olds tested by the Manchester team, however, went up only from 98.61 in 1989 to 99.59 in 1996, a rise which Miss Davies says is not statistically significant.

'If we are right then billions of pounds have been wasted and national tests do not do the job they are supposed to do'

Tests on seven-year-olds in the same schools found a similar lack of improvement.

The study was carried out with eight classes of seven and 11-year-olds from five schools in the city. It found they were doing less well than children nationally when the test was standardised in the early 1980s, with 100 being the mean score achieved by the age groups.

A spokesman for the School Curriculum and Assessment authority, which oversees the national tests, said it was difficult to draw conclusions from a small study.

'Children are also learning different things now from what was being taught in schools in the early 1980s,' she said.

'They are covering a much broader maths curriculum and the national curriculum tests are more wide-ranging. We are confident that our tests are robust because of the amount of research and development which has gone into them.'

She admitted, however, that part of the improvements shown in the national tests over recent years could be due to the growing willingness of teachers to revise work with the children. 'Revision used to be a dirty word in education but we would maintain it is an important and useful educational tool,' she said.

Righting reading

British children could and should be more literate

Standards of literacy in this country are shockingly low. Only half of all 11-year-olds reach the level that virtually all should be able to achieve. Without the basic ability to read and write, children of that age cannot cope with secondary school and may then be blighted for life.

So it is encouraging that the Government is concentrating so hard on the three Rs – and particularly on remedial education for the long tail of underachievers in our school system. Yesterday Stephen Byers, Minister for Standards, launched a pilot scheme of literacy summer schools for those who are a couple of years behind their reading age at 11. Pupils will have intensive tuition with some individual attention and a healthy injection of fun alongside the work.

For many children who are lagging at this age, such summer camps could make the difference between an easy and a difficult transition to secondary school. The move from a small primary school to a huge secondary can be traumatic enough without the alienation of being unable to follow the lessons properly. Too many children drop out at this stage and turn to truancy and crime. A network of summer schools could help to motivate many underachievers. But there is still the problem of the bottom 20 per cent who are too far behind to catch up with just two weeks of intensive help. Their problems need to be addressed far earlier in their school careers.

At seven, the disparity between the highest and lowest achievers is far smaller than at 11. In the seven-year-old tests, only 20 per cent of pupils fail to achieve the results expected for their age. This percentage doubles by the end of primary school.

In New Zealand, a concentration on literary has enabled 80 per cent of children to read well through normal teaching. A further 15 per cent catch up after an intensive Reading Recovery programme starting at six. Only 5 per cent still have reading problems by the end of primary school.

Without the basic ability to read and write, children of age 11 cannot cope with secondary school and may then be blighted for life

Britain needs to improve both the general teaching of literacy and the remedial effort put into those who fall behind. Mr Blunkett's emphasis on phonics, in which children are taught the relationship between letters and sounds, and his advocacy of a 'literacy hour' in school each day, should help to improve the skills of the majority. Then the minority needs to be addressed.

First, teachers need to understand why children fail to learn to read. Although there is some correlation between test results and deprivation, there is still a huge variation between schools with a similar social intake. So, for instance, primary schools with the most deprived pupils range from a 70 per cent success rate at 11-year-old English tests to 0 per cent. Poverty and lack of parental support have become alibis behind which ineffective teachers and schools learn to hide. But with good teaching, most children from any social background can succeed.

As well as being offered remedial help, underachievers could benefit from a less rigid obsession with chronological age. Tony Blair has already suggested that able children should be accelerated through school. The converse should be allowed for those who need more time to grasp the basics. In many continental countries, children who fall behind are expected to repeat a year. If this were done here at the age of seven, more children would leave primary school with the critical skills necessary to cope with the next stage of their life.

Labour turns its back on years of 'trendy' teaching

By Dorothy Lepkowska, Education Correspondent

Labour was today discarding three decades of trendy education theories in favour of traditional methods and tough new targets to raise standards in Britain's schools.

In its first education White Paper, hailed by Education Secretary David Blunkett as a 'framework for achievement', the Government was bringing back streaming, accelerated learning for gifted children and whole-class teaching. The proposals signal a huge departure for Labour and acknowledge the comprehensive system has failed.

Although Mr Blunkett has pledged no expansion of selection, his new proposals will no longer hold back the bright pupils whose achievements were stifled under progressive teaching. The main focus will be on underachievement and the problems faced by declining and failing inner-city schools. Plans include:

- A 'cash-for-results' scheme, with more funds for schools making big improvements in examinations, and attendance;
- The creation of 25 'action zones' to get additional funding and better teachers in a bid to raise standards;
- An elite group of teachers to turn around failing schools;
- Accelerated procedures for dismissing incompetent heads and teachers;
- A requirement that schools set development plans including tough targets for academic success;
- Monitoring by local authorities, which will answer directly to the Secretary of State if schools are seen to be failing.

Local authorities will also be given responsibility for publishing league tables, which will show how schools have improved or declined over three years.

The White Paper gives ministers unprecedented powers to intervene if standards are not met.

Mr Blunkett reiterated his 'zero tolerance' of failure today. He said: 'We are constructing a framework, which will achieve our goal of high quality and high standards of education for all our children.'

However, his plans are already causing conflict with teachers. The unions are angry that they may not be represented on a proposed General Teaching Council, and he is being accused of interfering with classroom practice.

Nigel de Gruchy, general secretary of the second largest teaching union, the NASUWT, said: 'Mr Blunkett should now show some faith in the ability of teachers to run their classes the best way according to the resources available on the ground.'

The shadow education secretary, Stephen Dorrell, said Labour's plans had echoes of Conservative policies.

He said: 'Improving standards is partly about testing and assessment, but it is also about ensuring that the profession has the freedom to teach its own ideas, and that parents have a proper opportunity to choose between schools.'

Prime Minister Tony Blair, today visiting literacy classes and watching a school concert rehearsal with Mr Blunkett, said: 'Our commitment to education is not negotiable.

'I want the best for all our schoolchildren to make Britain truly competitive into the next millennium.'

The Government's targets to the year 2002

Early years	Nursery education for all four-year-olds who want it Testing of all children starting primary school Classes of fewer than 30 for five, six and seven-year-olds One hour a day devoted to literacy and numeracy in every primary school Training for teachers in literacy and numeracy teaching methods
Standards	League tables to show rate of progress of schools Each school to have its own targets Failing schools to close, or given 'fresh start' Ofsted to begin inspections of local authorities
Comprehensives	Schools to set pupils by ability Education Action Zones to provide support to inner-city trouble spots Network of specialist schools Better infotmation and communications technology
Teaching	First-time heads to hold a professional headship qualification Additional training for existing heads Better training in teaching methods in literacy, numeracy and information technology A new grade of Advanced Skills Teacher More efficient procedures for dealing with incompetant teachers A General Teaching Council to speak for and promote the profession
Home and School	A home-school contract in all schools Greater representation of parents on governing bodies Better support for pupils with behaviour problems and fewer exclusions Reduced levels of truancy No children missing out on GCSEs by leaving school early National guidelines for homework and creation of after-school clubs
Partnership	New framework of foundation, community and aided schools Fair systems for calculating school budgets Fairer ways of allocating school places Improved partnership between state and independent sectors

Chicago gets tough with its dunces

Beset by appalling results from its schools, Chicago has adopted radical techniques which are attracting international attention. By Mary Dejevsky

As school-leavers in England and Wales contemplate the arrival today of their career-determining A-level results and teachers gird themselves for the inevitable debate about standards, they might spare a thought for their counterparts across the Atlantic, in Chicago. Here, a daring, perhaps desperate, experiment is under way which is intended to raise standards in a city long reputed to have the worst school system in America.

Education officials in Chicago deny that their schools were ever the worst. They admit that they might not have been centres of national excellence, but say they were only among the worst. The label – bestowed by Ronald Reagan's education secretary, William Bennett – stuck none the less. Now the city is in the throes of a system-wide reform that is attracting attention from school departments across the US and even from Britain. Education officers from Birmingham have been over to take a look.

The Chicago experiment derived from a realisation that many pupils were leaving school without even the bare essentials to be employable. True, the city had a special problem; by the early 1990s, the flight of the white middle class to the suburbs had left the city's schools with an overwhelming majority of children from poor, mainly ethnic 'minority' homes. Some 54 per cent of today's pupils are black; another 30 per cent Hispanic.

The Chicago experiment derived from a realisation that many pupils were leaving school without even the bare essentials to be employable

But when a new mayor, Richard Daley – son of the long-serving major-baron of Chicago, 'Joe' Daley – was elected in 1995, he pledged to re-vamp the city's education. Too many people, he said, had written off the pupils as doomed to fail. It was the schools that were failing, and the city was failing the schools.

Whatever is said about Mayor Daley, and much of it even from political opponents is positive, he has fulfilled his promise to shake up the schools. Seven are being 'reconstituted' – with a new head and all staff required to reapply for their jobs. One in five of the city's 550 schools are 'on probation': they are being monitored, that is, by the education department, until they improve either their financial management or educational and attendance standards.

Mayor Daley's initial achievement was to have the state of Illinois, which formerly appointed the city's school board, cede control of schools and their huge, $2.8bn (£1.6bn) budget to Chicago. He then pruned and recast the administration, appointing a chief executive and a finance chief, who together turned a big deficit into a small surplus within a year. Some of that is being used for long-delayed repairs and refurbishment. Of five schools I visited, four were in the midst of extensive works. Perhaps the biggest undertaking, however, is the city's determination to improve standards,

above all the pupils' test scores. Chicago pupils, along with most US children, take national tests of basic skills – reading and mathematics – at crucial points in their school careers. In the past, the scores were recorded, lamented – and largely disregarded. The pupils went automatically into the next grade, and lagged further and further behind.

Last year, for the first time, eighth-graders (14-year-olds) who did not reach the standard set by the city were not allowed to go on to high school (the four-year school leading to a diploma). They had to go to special summer classes to try to improve their scores. More than half did.

The others, to widespread consternation, had to stay down a year. If by then they had passed their fifteenth birthday, they were deemed too old to return to grade school, and were placed in a 'transitional centre' for special classes designed to help them catch up with their year group within a year. Some 1,100 pupils were placed in these centres last year.

At the end of this academic year, the programme, known as the 'Summer Bridge', became compulsory not just for failed eighth-graders, but for three other year groups, older and younger. In all, more than 10 per cent of the city's 420,000 pupils were required to attend the special seven-week programme, and in some schools the number exceeded 50 per cent.

Staffed by selected teachers, all experienced and well regarded (and paid for the additional 'term'), the summer programmes do not attempt to repeat the school year at speed. They use special course materials, chosen for 'relevance' and soundness, comprising a mix of original work and 'rote' learning that would please both the 'learn by doing' and the 'back to basics' tendencies.

Officials at the city's education department stress that the reform is not just about improving test scores or Chicago's position in the national scale. It is mainly about pupils and equipping them for the world beyond school. It is also an attempt to break with two decades of rampant 'grade inflation', when teachers felt under pressure to pass every child, regardless of achievement, and the 'social' benefits of keeping children in their year group were thought to outweigh individual educational achievement.

It is too early to judge the results of the reforms, but first indications are good. Test scores in the last academic year were the best this decade. Karen Morris, head at a predominantly Hispanic school in the south of the city, said that there had been a clear change in pupils' attitudes once they understood that they would be kept down if they failed. They were, she said, 'much more focused this year'.

An education official responsible for overseeing the summer programme also noted one of the by-products of the back-to-basics approach and said he favoured much more of it. If a parent comes in complaining that his or her child has failed and that is unfair for whatever reason, he said, 'I can call in the child and ask him, "What is six times seven?" or whatever, and if he can't answer, I can tell the parent. "You see, he doesn't know his times tables."' Without that requirement for specific knowledge the parent could say the child was just a poor test-taker or felt unwell on the day.

There are dissenters from the new approach. Some were involved with previous attempts to improve education in Chicago. They complain that the present administration is actually reaping a harvest that was sown by previous reformers and say that the roller-coaster of the past decade has damaged teachers' morale and confused parents and pupils.

Some dissenters, however, are now converts. Sitting in his cramped un-air-conditioned office, with the fan on full blast, one head of year said he was already seeing the benefits in pupils' attitude and achievement. And sometimes it is the small things that count. The provision of brand-new textbooks and calculators for this year's compulsory summer courses, in sufficient numbers for each pupil to have their own, was itself a morale-booster for teachers and pupils, said Angela Murdoch, director of one of the programmes at a big problem-ridden school in northern Chicago. They were so used to being at the bottom of the pile.

This week, Chicago's compulsory summer pupils will have been awaiting their results with as much trepidation as Britain's A-level candidates. Whether the compulsory summer programme element of the Chicago school reform would transfer to Britain, however, is another matter. How many parents, or children, would forego their holidays to spend another seven weeks at school? In Chicago, every teacher told me, this was the least of their problems: as one put it: 'There's not a lot of people here going to Florida.'

Dearing decides on 'least bad plan' for tuition fees

Government offers another proposal, but leaves committee no time to judge it

By John Carvel, Education Editor

Sir Ron Dearing yesterday produced what he believed was the least bad plan for introducing tuition fees for full-time undergraduates. It would not have answered all the universities' funding worries, but he thought it came nearest to meeting a national need to produce more graduates without putting an intolerable burden on taxpayers, students or their parents.

Within two hours the Government announced a different proposal, which resembled one of Sir Ron's discarded alternatives but was different enough to require reworking the figures from scratch before the committee could judge it.

The government plan was not conveyed to Sir Ron until last week, too late for him to analyse the numbers on a sophisticated computer model set up for the purpose.

What is left is a report giving detailed analysis of what the Government says it does not want to do and only sketchy details of the consequences of what it prefers.

The Dearing committee accepted the principle that 'the costs of higher education should be shared among those who benefit'. But if the burden on graduates was too great, this would discourage applications from more disadvantaged students – the very people institutions need to attract to make the system fairer and achieve Sir Ron's growth target.

The report analysed proposals in the Labour manifesto to scrap the means-tested student maintenance grant which provides poorer students with up to £2,160 a year to meet about half their living costs.

Under the manifesto option these grants would have been converted into long-term loans, repayable after graduation by instalments linked to income. There was no mention of tuition fees, but poorer students would have graduated after a three-year course up to £6,500 more in debt.

Sir Ron found this proposal failed to meet any of his objectives. It 'took away subsidies from the poorest families' and redirected them towards the rich who would have been given more convenient methods of repayment over a longer timescale. There would have been no saving on public spending over the next few years and surprisingly little over the long term.

'We have concluded that any option which delivered the resources needed would produce unacceptable burdens on graduates,' the report said.

Having dismissed the policy on which Labour fought the election, the committee advanced its own preference. This would have kept the maintenance grant at current rates, but introduced a flat-rate tuition fee of about £1,000 a year – covered by a similar income-contingent loan repayable after graduation.

There would have been no exemptions for students from poor families because repayments would depend on the graduate's eventual earnings and not on family background. The committee thought the fee could yield about £1.1 billion in the long term.

This posed two big problems for David Blunkett, the Education and Employment Secretary. It would involve abandoning the manifesto line and would raise only about half the money needed for the universities and colleges.

Mr Blunkett said yesterday he wanted to build on the Dearing plan, but in effect he threw it out and started from scratch. The grant would be abolished, but students from families on incomes below £16,000 would be exempt from tuition fees and those earning up to £34,000 would get partial relief.

Poorer students would graduate up to £6,500 more in debt – just as they would under the manifesto plan – and richer students would graduate £3,000 more in debt.

Under the government plan repayments would not start on incomes below £10,000. The average graduate on a salary of £19,000 would pay about £55 a month, compared with up to £87 a month under the existing student loan scheme. Poor graduates could take up to 23 years to pay their debt.

These figures do not tell the whole story because they do not focus on the position of the poor student with above-average debt. Extra hardship loans of up to £250 a year will also have to be repaid.

Mr Blunkett's plan may raise £1.7 billion compared with Sir Ron's £1.1 billion, but most of the extra will come from poorer students whom the reforms are meant to lure to university.

> ***Poorer students would graduate up to £6,500 more in debt and richer students would graduate £3,000 more in debt***

The cost of an education

Student whose parents earn under £16,000

Name: Nicholas Honey
Age: 21
Subject: Software engineering at Newcastle University. Just completed second year.
Maintenance Grant: Maximum outside London grant of £1,755.
Govt. maintenance loans: £1,385 in first year; £1,645 for second year and expecting to take out same loan for final year.
Other loans: None.
Time to pay back loan: When I get a job earning over £13,000. Five years to pay off loan.
Estimated debt when leaving university: £7,000

Under the Dearing plan
Nicholas would keep his grant and would get an extra government loan to cover the new £1,000-a-year tuition fee. This would increase his debt on graduation to £10,000, but repayments would depend on income and could be spread over 10 years.

Under the government plan
Parents' income low enough for Nicholas to escape the tuition fee. He'd lose his grant, but get the same amount of money in an extra loan. This would increase his debt on graduation to about £12,000, but he could spread repayments up to 23 years if he could not afford to settle more quickly. Ministers say repayments in early years could be less than now.

Student whose parents earn over £34,000

Name: Deborah Gold.
Age: 20.
Subject: Philosophy. Entering final year at Reading University.
Maintenance Grant: None (because parents earn too much). Parents contribute almost £1,800 per year.
Govt. maintenance loans: No loan in first year. Almost £1,800 for second year and around the same for final year.
Other loans: £700 bank overdraft. Expected to increase to £1,000 by time of leaving.
Time to pay back loan: When she starts work earning £13,000 plus.
Estimated debt when leaving university: £5,000

Under the Dearing plan
A student in Deborah's circumstances arriving at university after September next year would get an extra government loan to cover a £1,000-a-year tuition fee. No change in parental contribution. Repayment of government loans to start after graduation, on income as low as £5,000, but easy terms over 10 years.

Under the government plan
Same as Dearing, but repayment would start after graduation once income reached £10,000 and could be spread up to 23 years if her income stayed low.

Mature student

Name: Ann Fairhurst.
Age: 42.
Subject: Humanities. Just completed first year at Trent University.
Maintenance Grant: Maximum outside London grant of £1,755.
Govt. maintenance loans: £1,000 for first year. Planning for £800 loan for coming academic year.
Other loans: Planning to take small bank loan (around £500) to cover for summer vacation.
Time to pay back loan: I have been told that I have to start paying back my bank loan as soon as I leave university. Paying back the student loan company begins when I reach a salary of around £13,000. Five years to pay off loan once working.
Estimated debt when leaving university: £7,000

Under the Dearing plan
Ann would keep her grant, but government loans to cover maintenance and a £1,000-a-year tuition fee would become repayable after graduation once income reached £5,000. Annual repayments would depend on income, but could start as low as £50 a year, rising to about £2,250 when income topped £30,000.

Under the government plan
Since Ann's income was low enough to qualify for maximum grant, she would be exempted from the tuition fee, but would lose the maintenance grant of £1,755 a year. Debt and repayments: same as Nicholas.

Germany

One in three school-leavers goes on to university and higher education, with about 1.9 million higher education students in a country of 79 million.

Universities are mainly run by the federal states and funded from state budgets.

Half of students depend on parents for financial support, a quarter take out government loans, and many have jobs. University education is long – seven years is not unusual. A year's course fees total a little over £50.

Ian Traynor

Italy

About one in three Italians aged between 20 and 24 goes to university – although only about a third graduate.

Fees are payable on a means-tested basis, although most families pay less than £300. Another obstacle is the admission tests of some faculties.

Maintenance grants are available for those coming from home with low taxable incomes. Students have to get consistently high marks in exams to get grants.

John Hooper

Finland

Seventeen universities have a total student population of 80,000. About 20 per cent of school-leavers take the four or five-year degree course. Another 20 to 30 per cent start a vocational course.

Course fees are paid by the state. The basic maintenance grant is £170 a month for students aged 20 or over living independently; younger students receive less. Those away from home get a monthly housing grant of 67 per cent of their rent.

Jon Henley

France

Eighty-one per cent of pupils who passed the baccalauréat last year continued into higher education in 89 universities and in dozens of medical, art, business and engineering schools.

Tuition is free, though students must pay for lodging and food. The government calculates that it spends £3,300 a year on a university student and £7,800 on a future engineer. Grants are available for living costs.

Alex Duval Smith

Sixth-formers forced to pay to study for A-levels

Sixth-form colleges are charging students up-front fees of up to £120 to enrol for A-level courses although, by law, tuition must be free for students up to the age of 18. Lucy Ward and Louise Hancock found cash-strapped colleges asking parents to bail them out

More than two-thirds of sixth-form colleges are asking students to pay for registration fees or contribute towards books or examination costs, according to an *Independent* survey.

Though some are charging as little as £5 or £10, many more, particularly in affluent areas of the South-east, are asking for sums of £100 or more, generating tens of thousands of pounds annually for college funds.

Principles say they are levying charges or asking for named voluntary contributions with great reluctance, but insist they must find alternative sources of income when state funding is too low to protect quality. They protest that colleges are being expected to compete for students with school sixth forms despite receiving significantly lower funding.

The growing trend, which has seen dozens of sixth-form colleges introduce or raise charges or requests for contributions this term, is raising alarm among many principals.

They warn that 'hidden charging', which is not being monitored nationally, is concealing serious inadequacies in the funding of sixth-form education.

The issue will also raise questions for the Government over how far private individuals should be asked to subsidise state education. Ministers have already taken the decision to charge students for part of their university tuition fees from next year.

Legally, sixth-form colleges are not permitted to charge tuition fees for full-time students aged 16 to 18, but each institution is free to charge for registration, exam fees or books and other materials.

The Independent's survey of 60 colleges – just over half the total – revealed examples such as the College of Richard Colyer in Horsham, West Sussex, where students are asked to pay a £120 registration fee for their two-year course, and buy their own books and materials at an estimated cost of £26 a year.

The fee, up from £100 last year, brought in £60,000 this year, and the college saved £26,000 on books and materials. Charges are waived for low-income families.

Though some are charging as little as £5 or £10, many more, particularly in affluent areas of the South-east, are asking for sums of £100 or more

At the Sixth Form College, Farnborough, which gained one of the best inspection reports in the sector, new students paid a £100 registration fee this term. Dr John Guy, the principal, who has raised concerns over colleges' financial position with the Department for Education and Employment, said: 'College governors introduced the fee in order to protect the high quality of education demonstrated by our inspection report.'

The Further Education Funding Council, the quango which distributes funding to colleges, pledged yesterday to examine the growth of charging after being questioned on the trend by *The Independent*.

Managing on a shoestring

'Where did all the money go?' is an oft-heard cry from new students. By John Andrew

With celebrations of exam results still under way, you're already dreaming of your new-found freedom away from the family home – but the chances are you haven't yet given a thought to the financial aspects of your new lifestyle. Learning the monetary facts of life can be painful – and as a new student you'll be particularly vulnerable.

The chances are that until now you've lived all your life within the family environment. Then you are suddenly given a bank account and what's almost certainly the largest sum of money you have ever had and told to fend for yourself.

It's a far cry from managing your pocket-money. 'I've had a great time, but I just do not know where this term's money's gone,' was a remark overheard outside a lecture theatre. The words of a first-year student – spoken not at the end of term, but at the end of the second week.

There will always be irresponsible students – but even the cautious can find it tough when thrown into a new lifestyle. One of the problems is that you and your parents are entering the unknown. The starting-point for estimating the costs of university life is often the total level of state funding – the full grant and student loan. But this covers the absolute basics and ignores regional differences in the cost of the largest outlay in any student budget – accommodation.

So head for the phone. Ring the accommodation office or the students' union to discover the average rents or hall fees. After that, work out the cost of food, travel, laundry, toiletries, insurance, entertainment, books and equipment. Perhaps there is someone from the year above you at school who is now back at home after a first year as a

student. Invite them round – preferably when your parents are at home – and you can all learn from their experiences.

By now you should know the level of grant you will receive (if any), the parental contribution you are expecting and the maximum student loan for which they may apply. Bringing these parts of the equation together, you and your parents can see the overall picture. It is unlikely that income and estimated expenditure will balance. Can spending be cut, do they have savings, can you get a part-time job? By exploring the situation together, you will have a greater appreciation of the problems involved.

While parents like to do the best for their children, this has to be within their financial means. So you have to look for savings that will be comparatively painless. For instance, you don't have to buy every book on a reading list. You can save pounds by making use of the library and buying second-hand.

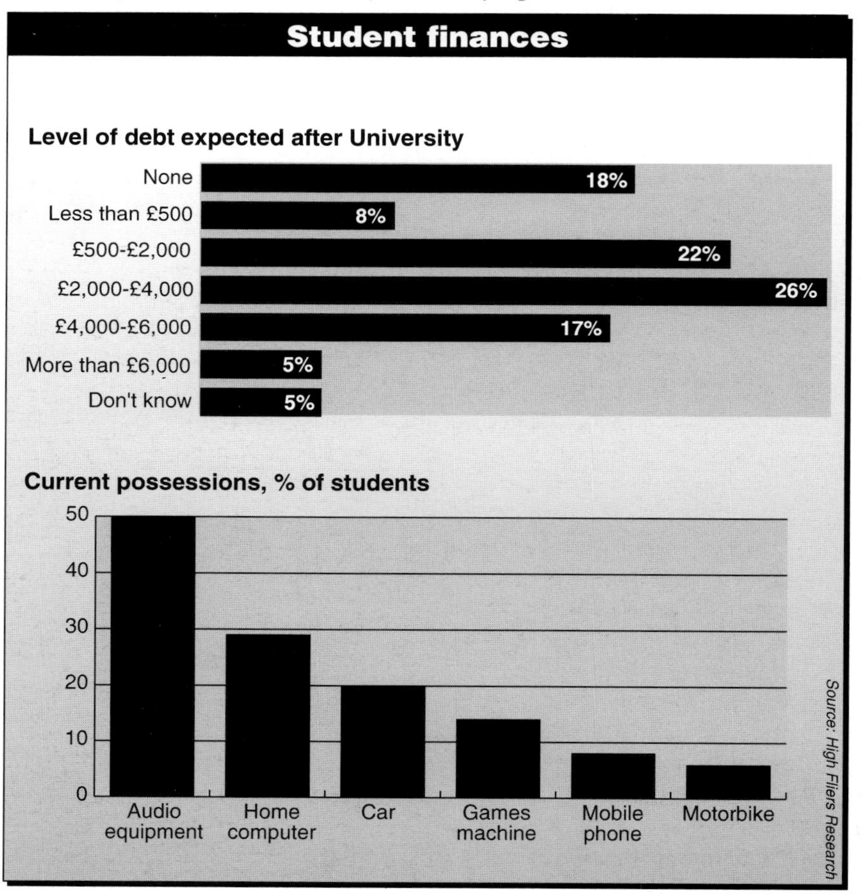

The last thing you may want is a lecture on how to budget. But you and your parents will benefit from detailed research and serious discussion.

Me & my budget

Making your money go further: three students tell Jean Carr and Ken Welsby how they juggle their finances.

Nazia Hirjee, 20, geography at St Hugh's, Oxford. Working as a 'temp' for two months of vacation. Has an annual grant of £1,710 and the maximum student loan of £2,420. Gets no financial help from her mother, who is a single parent.

I've just been on to my bank to increase my overdraft facility from £75 to the £1,100 I now owe them. They are very understanding but I'd like to complete my degree without panicking about money. The grant covers my hall residency fees, £470 a term, but really it's more like £550, as the term is so short. I need to stay in Oxford to use the libraries and prepare for next term. I don't buy new clothes, go on holiday, use the dining room or buttery and I walk everywhere. I cook my own food, that's £30 a week, and need £20 a week pocket money. My biggest expense is books, £80 to £100 a term, I'm not against the principle of borrowing, but I quibble at the amount. It's impossible to live on the full grant and student loan: I can't even cover my basic living costs without getting into debt. It affects the quantity, rather than quality, of my work. I'd like to spend more time studying in the holidays rather than working as a temp, and buy more books so I wouldn't have the expense of staying in Oxford to use the libraries. I'd like to consider postgraduate courses but the pressure when I graduate next year is to get a job to pay off debts.

John Cramner, 21, media studies at Westminster. Grant for last year was £1,680, which covered just over a third of his expenditure during term time. Has the maximum student loans – and a £500 overdraft.

This summer I'm staying in London to find work, but that means paying £750 in extra rent for my room in the house I share. Last summer I went home to Swavesey, sent off my CV to masses of people and got only one week's work, gardening, for £120. Bus fares cost £5 a day and I had to leave home at 5.30 am. In term-time my monthly expenditure is £233 rent, about £25 for household bills, food £48, pocket money £84 and clothes about £20. I go through periods when I am completely overdrawn and mum's contribution is usually a month's rent each term. But some of my friends are worse off. Fortunately we live within walking distance of the campus and Tesco. We always eat at home. I can't go to as many films or music events as I'd like to, or buy as many records as I want, you can't really ask your parents to pay for things like that. I buy new clothes only when I am working – usually doing picture returns for magazines. Last year I earned £3,000 which was brilliant, but that work has dried up now. When I finish next summer I will owe the full £5,000 in student loans and whatever my overdraft will be. So I must find a job as soon as possible.

Jane Edwards, 21, history at Liverpool. Gets £600 a month from her parents in term time – of which £300 goes in rent and utility bills. Spends most of her vacations in the family business – providing secretarial and clerical holiday cover.

I'm luckier than a lot of people in that my family are supporting me – and of course the business pays me in vacations. It's real work and it pays a real wage: almost £900 a month after tax. I live at home with the folks when I'm working because my flatmate Beth and I are keeping our flat all year round. Books are the biggest lump sum in my budget; in my first year I was lucky and found about half of them second-hand, but last year I had to get all of them new. That was £126 in not much more than an hour. I try to budget carefully: Beth and I each put £18 a week into the housekeeping – plus a tenner from our boyfriends because they eat with us a couple of times in the week and at weekends. You've got to trust people when you're sharing – our only real horror story has been with one phone bill. My boyfriend spent ages on the phone trying to arrange a work and study trip to Eastern Europe – we thought the calls had cost £40, but when the bill came it was more like £100! But we wouldn't like to be without a phone, it's great to be able to keep in touch with home.

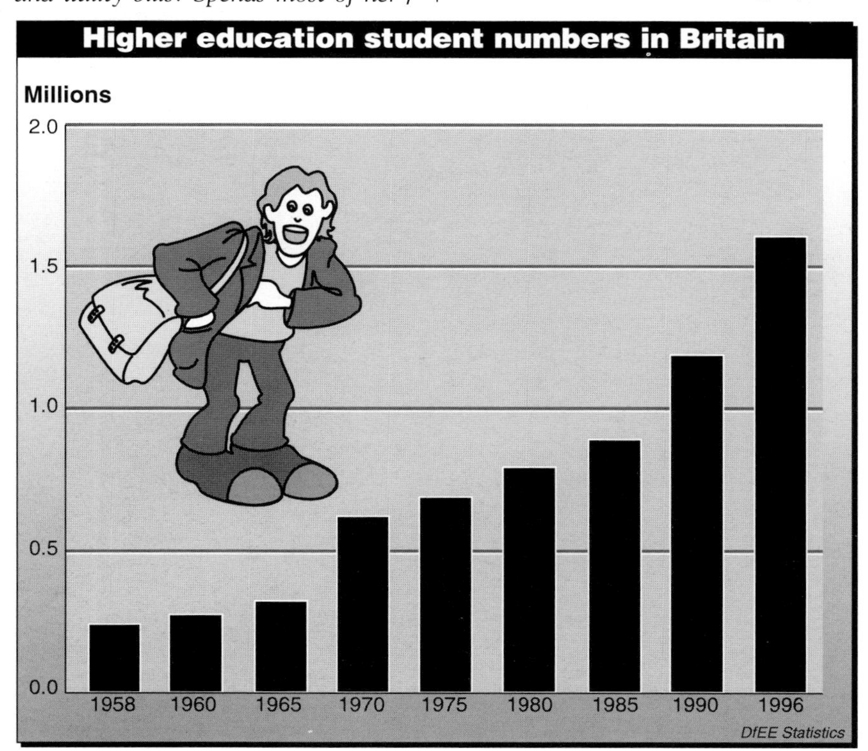

How to top up the grant

Learning to live on a budget is one of the biggest challenges of student life. Individual budgets will depend on the size of your bills and your personal spending – but here come some tips from those who have had to learn the hard way how to make their money stretch

By Beryl Dixon

Grants are down: debt is up. If you want to avoid going into the red as much as possible you will need to tap every possible source of finance. What are they? First comes the grant – if you get one. Most of you will know by now how much you are going to receive from your local education authority.

If you have not yet applied for a grant the message is to do so at once. You have up to four months after the start of your course in which to do so, but presumably you will want the money before then.

The next major source is the student loan. There is no shame in applying for one. The Government expects that you will. The grant figure has been decreasing and the loan increasing for some years. For the first time the two figures are almost equal. It is a cheap way of borrowing money and you don't have to repay it until the April after you finish your course. If your salary then is less than 85 per cent of national average earnings, repayment can be deferred.

You cannot apply for a loan until you start your course and forms will be available at your university or college. You may make only one application a year but the money can be paid in three instalments to help you to budget. Some students take the full amount and put it in an interest-bearing account. Others put off applying for a loan until they need to do so. Before you choose the first method, ask yourself two questions:

- Can you trust yourself not to blow it all at once?
- Can you find a good rate of interest?

More students than ever now have part-time jobs and gone are the days when this was frowned upon

The full grant figures for students starting their courses next month are: £2,160 if living away from home and studying in London, £1,755 if studying elsewhere and £1,435 for those living with their parents. Maximum loan figures for this year are £2,085, £1,685 and £1,290. The grant is, of course, reduced according to your family's income.

If your parents can't help much or you are a mature student you are almost certainly – given that most institutions estimate that you will need over £4,000 to survive three terms – going to need more. So where will it come from? Quite a bit from yourself probably! More students than ever now have part-time jobs and gone are the days when this was frowned upon. Many students work for about 12 hours a week in term time. The places to try are the same ones you may have worked in already at weekends – pubs, clubs, supermarkets.

One tip is to get a reference from your home employer and look for a job at a branch in your new area. Try your new careers service too. Many have noticeboards displaying part-time jobs and some even display vacancies from the Jobcentre.

You may not have to leave the campus. Students' Unions have always been a good source of bar, catering and even office work but now some university and college authorities make conscious efforts to reserve jobs for students – as cleaners, porters, gardeners and refectory assistants. Some students find work in the libraries and offices.

Rates of pay are generally £3-£5 per hour, but you could earn more than this if you have a marketable skill. Think hard. Can you teach a musical instrument? Coach school-children in maths or French? Could you qualify as a swimming teacher, sew or cook for other people? Some inventive students run mini businesses.

There are two further sources of grants and loans. The first is open to most people. It's called a bank overdraft, is offered by all banks (amounts vary) but must be treated with caution. While the banks offer students an interest-free overdraft up to a certain limit, charges apply once you overstep that. You must visit the bank to organise one. They will probably want to see details of your outgoings and your budget. Most branches near higher education establishments have student officers, specially trained to help. It pays to establish good relationships with them – and not to let things get out of hand before consulting them!

The second source is your institution's Access Fund. This is a sum they receive out of which they can assist students at their discretion. They could give you a grant of £100 or several thousand but the larger amounts are given only in cases of extreme hardship. If you think you might be eligible for a payment ask at the registry or welfare office.

Facts and figures on life on a budget

Claire Briggs lives in a hall of residence. As she is studying textiles, she has to buy extra equipment which typically costs between £5-£10.

Her budget looks like this:

Hall fees	£61
Snacks	£10
Laundry	£1
Toiletries	£2
Books and equipment	£5-£10
Clothes	£10
Weekly travel	£5
Entertainment	£20-£30
Miscellaneous (Stamps, stationery)	£2
Total	*£116-£131*

Claire's tips:

- Buy second-hand clothes
- Bring as many toiletries from home as you can
- Make sure you bring cutlery and crockery to make your own light meals and snacks

Dominic Hart lives in university-owned self-catering accommodation, in which he pays £35 rent plus £3 for electricity.

His expenditure breaks down as follows:

Rent	£35
Electricity	£3
Main meals and snacks	£16
Toiletries and household items	£1
Books and equipment	£1
Clothes	£5
Weekly travel	£2
Entertainment	£10
Miscellaneous (CDs, presents etc)	£12
Total	*£85*

Dominic's tips:

- Use self discipline
- Buy cheap brands
- Cook in groups and share expenses
- Scrounge more from home

Clea Sambrook, Michael Holland, Nadia Foley-Comer, Lauren Samuel and Justine Want share a house in Brighton, and split the bills in five equal shares.

Phone rental – shared (each pays for own calls)

Electricity – metered (take it in turn to put money in)

Food and drink – each buys own

Loo rolls, cleaning materials etc: bought when needed and cost shared

Household budgets are as follows:

Rent	£43.50
Gas	£6-£7
Electricity	£2
Phone	£4
Television rental	£1.40
Food	£20
Approx Total	*£78*

Figure based on a 30-week academic year, and do not include personal and social spending. Quarterly bills are shared, so the total includes some allowance for extra weeks when they may not stay in Brighton

Summer, 1997

Now work out your own . . .

Total weekly income
grant, loan, parents,
part-time earnings £ ________

Weekly outgoings

Rent	£ ________
Gas & electricity	£ ________
Food	£ ________
Books and equipment	£ ________
Clothes	£ ________
Fares	£ ________
Toiletries etc	£ ________
Presents – Christmas etc	£ ________
Total	£ ________
Remainder (to spend!!!)	£ ________

The first week

It's exciting, it's new, you're a fresher. How long you keep this label varies from place to place – sometimes the first term; sometimes longer. Caroline Marshall reports

Nearly every university and college organises a programme known as Freshers' Week or Intro Week. It may actually be a few days rather than a full week unless you are a mature student or coming from overseas, in which case there are often special days organised which are timed to end as all the other freshers arrive.

It's essential to go early for Freshers' Week. Not only do you meet people and find out which clubs and societies you want to join – good for meeting other new students and ones from other years – but you will have necessary administrative details to attend to.

The details will obviously vary, but on the right there's a quick rundown of some of the things you will have to do during the first week of your course. The week is sometimes arranged by the university or college authorities, but more often by the students' union officers who organise volunteer second and third-year students to come back early and run events.

It may or may not include talks from various people who are there to provide help in different circumstances – advisers, counsellors, welfare officers, medical centre staff, careers service. If they don't appear during the freshers' programme, you will certainly receive information about them in your students' handbook.

The first few days are exciting. They will give you the opportunity to find your way around and to make new friends – but they can also be confusing.

You might feel slightly lost, or even, to your great surprise, homesick. Don't worry. Nearly everyone else – even the confident-looking type in the next room – is in the same boat.

- Enrol for your course, meet lecturers and your personal tutor
- Enrol at the library and computing centre
- Register with the institution's health service or with a local doctor
- Get your Student Union identity card – this not only lets you into Union events, but usually brings discounts from shops, eating places, cinemas, hairdressers, travel companies and so on
- Open a bank account, unless you have one already – in which case you might want to transfer your account to the local branch
- Buy some books
- Have a guided tour of the campus
- Try out for sports teams that interest you
- Collect your grant cheque and apply for a student loan.

Survival tips

- Make sure you have a supply of tea and coffee. You can be the one to break the ice and offer cups to others on your corridor if you are in hall
- Take things to remind you of home
- Make sure you have enough money to last the first few days. Remember that grant cheques may be delayed.

I wish I had known . . .

Students look back on some of the things they wish they had known at the start of their courses

- How to budget efficiently
- How to balance a social life with my workload
- How to handle the lack of privacy in Hall
- How to motivate myself into

getting up in the morning to go to lectures I know will be boring
- How to make the most of the library facilities
- How to study effectively after a year out
- How to cope with commuting to the university every day – and not have my own car

Amanda Forsyth
Manchester Metropolitan University

- The change from working at A-level to working at degree level
- What the accommodation would be like
- How many extension leads I would need
- What the new people would be like
- Advance information about societies to join
- How easy it is to avoid work
- That drinking too much causes tummy upsets

Sian Thomas
Lancaster University

- How to manage money
- How to organise my work with all this new-found independence
- All the time I would have to myself
- That I should make the most of it because the terms go so quickly
- That I would miss my friend so much
- How mentally demanding a degree can be
- Not to have too many high expectations
- That given time I will settle in and that it will take a lot longer than three terms

Tatiana Simon, Manchester Metropolitan University

- That self-motivation can be difficult
- How much washing powder to use when washing clothes
- How to type
- How to consume vast amounts of alcohol without being ill
- How to manage time and money
- How to read certain texts without feeling sleepy
- Academic jargon
- How to tolerate arrogant public school boys

Michael Holland
Sussex University

- How much work I would be expected to do
- Whether I would be living in mixed accommodation
- What my accommodation would be like
- How much I would have to adjust to independence and freedom
- How much money I would need
- The possibilities for different sports and the level of competence needed
- What a lecture would be like
- What the town's pubs and shops would be like
- How much alcohol people would consume

Dominic Hart
Lancaster University

• This information is by UCAS. See page 41 for address details.

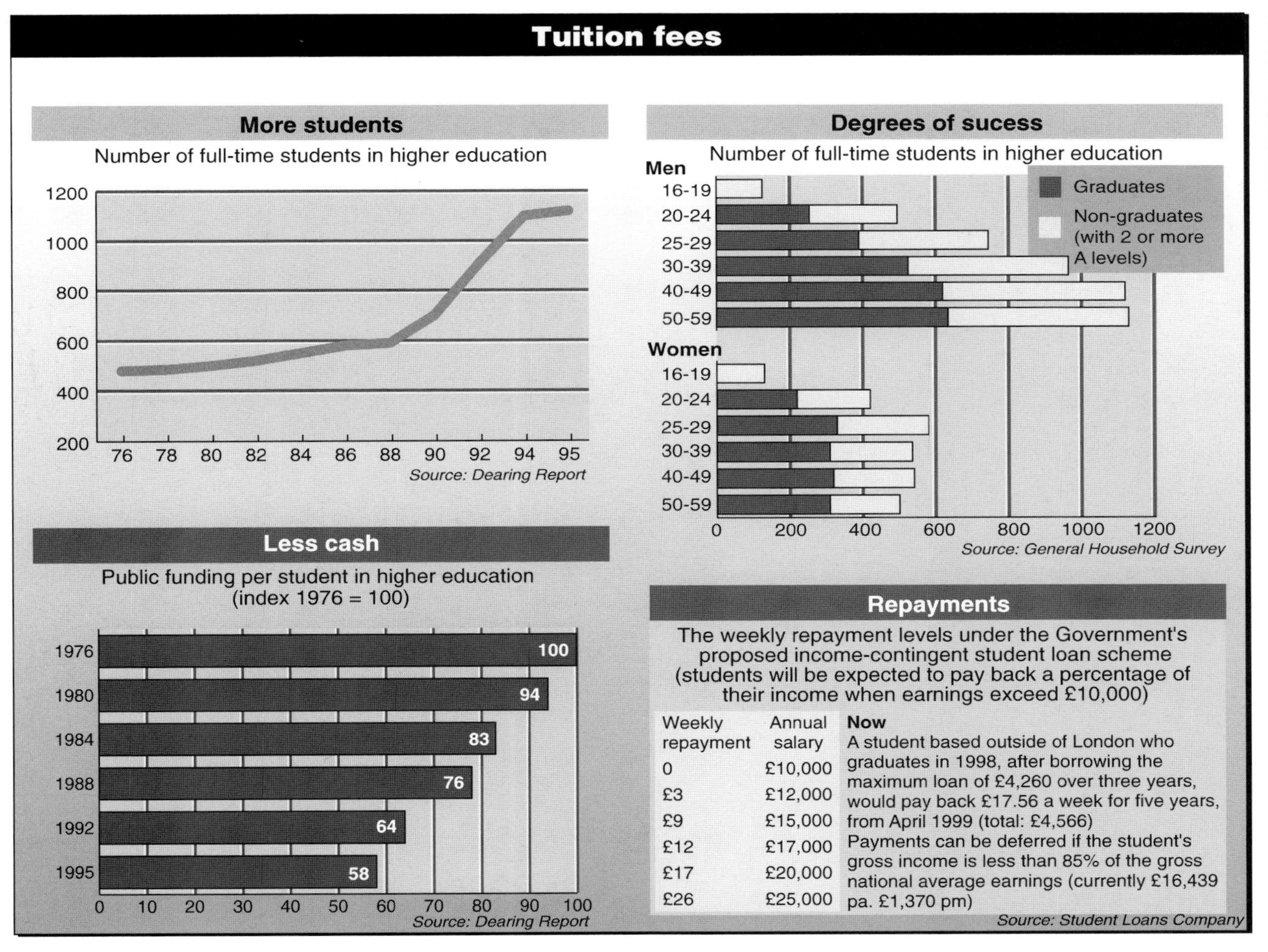

Weekly repayment	Annual salary
0	£10,000
£3	£12,000
£9	£15,000
£12	£17,000
£17	£20,000
£26	£25,000

Now
A student based outside of London who graduates in 1998, after borrowing the maximum loan of £4,260 over three years, would pay back £17.56 a week for five years, from April 1999 (total: £4,566)
Payments can be deferred if the student's gross income is less than 85% of the gross national average earnings (currently £16,439 pa. £1,370 pm)

Source: Student Loans Company

Making it stretch

Students work miracles every day in stretching every penny, and it will not take you long to discover that you can live a lot more cheaply than you think

Leaving home and trying to cope practically and financially for the first time can be a real headache, even for students who have been quite independent. Yes, you can cook but does that mean putting a packet in the microwave or blowing a week's housekeeping on one special recipe? Can you feed yourself on a tight budget for a week?

You already pay for your own clothes and entertainment – but you can no longer buy those trainers or go to that club thinking. 'It's my money. I earned it.' Yes, you did, but you won't be living at home now. The money has to go further.

After those depressing thoughts – the good (or relatively good) news. You can live a lot more cheaply than you might think. You can't double your grant or print money but you will soon become an expert at deciding what is essential and what you can live without. Students work miracles in stretching every penny to its limits and finding ways of cutting costs.

How? Survive on second-hand clothes or ask for major items as presents. Seek out food bargains from supermarkets late in the evening or from market stalls. Buy in bulk with friends. Learn to cook cheaply. (Ask for a cookery book as a leaving home present.)

One unanimous piece of advice from old hands is not to rush out and buy every book on your reading list. You will soon find which are essential, which can be borrowed from the library or shared with friends – and when you first arrive at college or university you may be able to buy some second-hand. What else can you do?

- Frequent campus bars and discos: prices will be cheaper than in town
- Set yourself a cash limit for an evening out – and don't exceed it. Leave your credit card and cheque book behind
- Avoid joining too many clubs and societies in the first week. They all have joining fees and you won't have time for many
- Get a bicycle and avoid daily fares
- Invest in student rail and coach cards
- Use all the student discounts from retailers

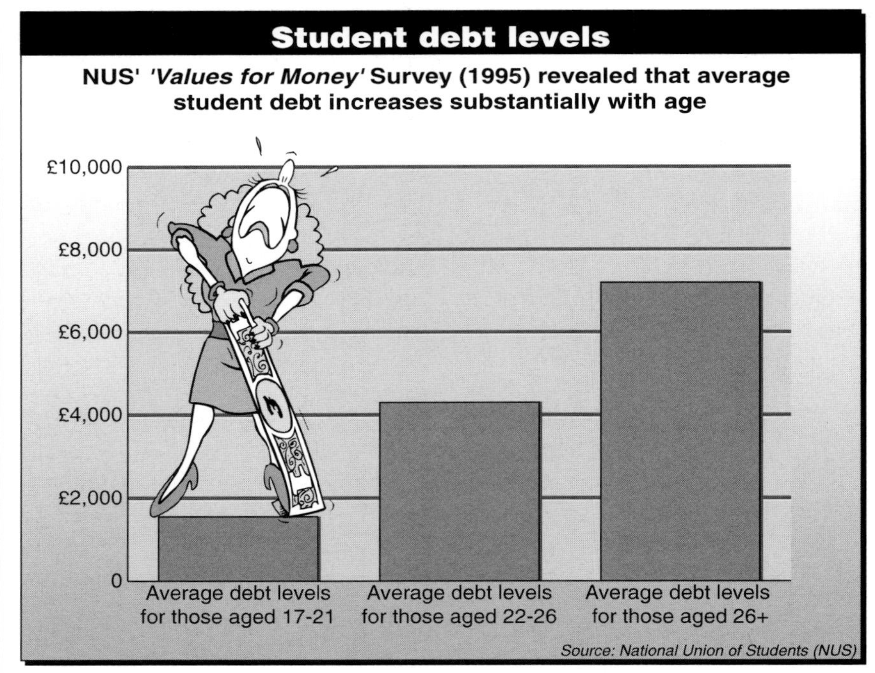

Whatever you spend, it is important that you know where it is going. You'll need to draw up a budget, which need not be complicated.

Unless, like Scrooge, you adore poring over figures, something simple will do. Some people prefer to budget in months; others find that it is safer to work in weeks.

Don't forget that if you take a year off your budget will have to be reworked in the wake of the Government's recent proposals for institutions to charge tuition fees and replace grants with further loans.

One thing you must allow for – unless it is included in hall fees or your parents take it out for you – is insurance. Student residences can be targets for undesirable types looking for computers, hi-fi and TV sets.

Finally, when you are working out how much money you have, do be sure that there has not been any communication gap.

The president of one students' union told of a first-year student who 'always had money and was incredibly generous'. When she asked her parents for money for the spring term it transpired that what they had given her in the autumn had supposedly been for the whole year!

You might also like to invest in *Students' Money Matters*, published by Trotman, £7.95.

Ready to foot the bill?

Many parents do not realise how much they may have to contribute to college costs, says Tony Lyons

If your child is going to university or college next month, are you ready to foot the bill? Many parents of the 800,000 or so students heading for higher education will be unprepared for the costs involved. If you haven't worked it out by now, there's no time to delay. Latest estimates are that, if your child decides not to take out the loans, it will cost around £15,000 to £18,000 for a three-year-degree course.

The maximum grant has been fixed for a number of years at £1,855 outside London and £2,340 in London for students living away from home. But that's fast becoming irrelevant, since fewer and fewer students qualify for any grant, let alone the full amount.

If their parents have a joint income of over £16,050, the grant is reduced. Earn more than £32,500 after allowances and they will get no grant at all. It is estimated that under a quarter of this year's intake will receive a full grant while as much as a third will get nothing at all.

All that will be covered by the state are tuition fees – and this year's intake is the last for which those will be fully paid. From 1998, students going into higher education will contribute around £1,000 a year, depending on parental income, towards the cost of tuition. This will be paid for by much higher interest-free student loans, which will only be paid back once the student is earning.

If your child is going to Liverpool or one of the other cheaper university towns, the National Union of Students estimates that they will need at least £4,300 a year.

More expensive towns will cost at least another £1,000 a year. Although the loans are designed to cover most expenditure, in practice they do not do so at the moment. Unless you had the foresight to start a savings plan early enough – and not many did – any contribution would have to be made out of income.

This could put a hefty dent in your salary. There are ways of reducing the impact but none of them is cheap. If there is sufficient free capital value in the house, it can be used to raise a first or second mortgage.

Some institutions offer special deals on money borrowed to pay for education. But you should expect to pay the going rate of interest. The Halifax, for example, has a drawdown loan that allows a minimum of £1,000 a time to be taken up to four times a year.

There is a £150 arrangement fee charged for setting up the scheme. Personal loans from a bank are another possibility, but relatively expensive – most charge at least 18 per cent interest.

A better option for those with gold credit cards is to use the low-cost loans that some offer. NatWest's gold card, for example, allows up to £10,000 to be borrowed with interest of 3 points over base rate, with a minimum charge of 10 per cent.

If you have a with-profits endowment policy, money can often be borrowed from your insurance company. Most insurers offer loans at reasonable rates, with the capital being repaid out of the policy's maturity value.

If you do not like the idea of borrowing money, and you cannot afford the student finance being paid out of income, then you will have to raise money by other means. For example, life assurance policies can be sold.

There are a number of firms now trading in second-hand policies who all tend to offer more than the surrender value paid by the insurer.

No matter how much you have to scrimp and scrape, it will always be worthwhile paying for your child's university life.

Student hardship affects families too

Information from the National Union of Students (NUS)

Reports of hardship amongst students have been prevalent in the press for a number of years. However, student hardship is arguably now a misnomer: as the demographic profile of students has aged – and many of these students have children – so whole families are affected by the low income which comes with being a full-time student.

At present a full-time undergraduate student with a married partner and two young children receives £4,435 in grant income and has the option of taking out a student loan up to a maximum of £1,645 per year. If her/his partner is not employed, s/he can claim social security benefits but may not receive anything – most of the student partner's grant income is taken into account as well as the loan even if it has not been taken out. So, this student family is expected to live on £117 per week – a third of which is a loan which has to be repaid (within five years) at the end of the course.

The scenario described above is not untypical. Twenty-nine per cent of entrants to full-time degree courses in 1996/97 were defined as immature; many of these have families. Yet income from the statutory student support system does not adequately reflect the needs of families with dependent children. Indeed, an additional component of the grant, payable to mature students (the older student allowance) which used to help students with families, was abolished in 1995.

A Department for Education and Employment (DfEE) commissioned student income and expenditure survey, conducted by the Policy Studies Institute during 1995/96 (*Student Finances: Income, Expenditure and take-up of Student Loans*, Policy Studies Institute 1996), found that mature students had higher spending levels than young students in all categories of expenditure with the exception of entertainment. Average total expenditure for mature students was £7, 502 per year. However, for mature students with dependent children this increased to £8,722 of which £1,976 was child-related expenditure. The latter figure breaks down as follows: £876 in direct childcare costs such as clothing and nursery/childminding fees, an extra £300 on housing costs, an extra £800 in living costs.

Lone parents owed, on average, £340 in arrears – more than 10 times the average amount for all students

Clearly, the dependants' additions to the grant (£405 per year for each child under the age of 11) come nowhere near covering these extra costs.

Additional costs are, of course, necessarily incurred just by entering education. The survey found that mature students incurred higher levels of course-related expenditure (such as books, equipment and computers) and higher spending on travel compared with young students.

It might be expected that the social security system would cushion student parent families against the hardship they would otherwise face when one – or even both – parents decides to enter full-time education. However, parents *per se* are not included in the list of vulnerable groups of students who can claim social security benefits. For the vast majority of students the social security system is not even available as a safety net when grant plus loan income is interrupted (due, for example, to sickness or exam failure).

The DfEE commissioned student income and expenditure survey found that lone-parent families fared even worse than two-parent families. Their average level of spending on children was £1,156 – one-third higher than the average for students overall. Moreover, their total expenditure – £9,849 – was by far the highest among any group of students. Indeed, the survey report

Annual student expenditure

	No children	Children	Lone parent
Essential expenditure			
Accommodation	1,653	1,954	2,258
Food/bills/household goods	1,471	2,296	2,757
Course expenditure	598	739	634
Essential travel	354	671	632
Children*	59	876	1,156
Other expenditure			
Entertainment	1,170	829	941
Non-essential travel	293	321	242
Other	652	743	1,035
Credit repayments	214	293	194
Total expenditure	£6,464	£8,722	£9,849

* Includes maintenance paid for children living with a former partner

Source: National Union of Students (NUS)

commented that on three indicators of financial strain, lone parents stand out in each category:

- 26 per cent of lone parents had received assistance from college access/hardship funds, compared with 6 per cent of all students;
- lone parents owed, on average, £340 in arrears – more than 10 times the average amount for all students;
- lone parents owed creditors [on average] a total of £3,148.

Lone parents rely, more than any other group of students, on state support (grant+loan+social security benefits) to finance their studies. They incur higher childcare costs than other students with children yet work, on average, far fewer hours (95 compared with an average of 143 hours engaged in paid work during the academic year for students overall).

It is not just the lack of financial support which is problematic for students with dependent children: finding their way around the complex regulations which apply to them also presents difficulties. Is any help available with paying the mortgage? What about childcare costs? How is child support maintenance dealt with by the awards regulations? Worst of all, some prospective students with dependent children are ill-informed or mis-advised: once they have entered education and discover they cannot cope financially it is often too late and they are forced to leave.

The survey report notes that for many lone parents education is a route out of dependence on state benefits. It can only be so if they have access to adequate financial support so that they are able to complete their courses successfully.

Student hardship hits record high

New survey shows students relying on parents to survive

The new report by Barclays Bank out today shows parents contribute an additional £403 million to their student children as levels of grant and loan fall far short of adequate funding.

This news comes on the eve of the Dearing report into higher education, due to be published later this month, which may call for students to pay tuition fees.

Douglas Trainer, NUS National President, said: 'The Barclays survey reveals the shocking reality of the state of student finance today. It is obvious that many students are only able to survive at college because of extra assistance from their parents, but clearly, this can't be the case for all students, especially those from low-income families. New suggestions that students should also bear the costs for their tuition are completely crushed by the facts revealed in the Barclays survey, proving the extent to which students and parents pay out now. The current system of student maintenance is failing students, graduates, parents and the taxpayer and needs reform urgently. Forcing students to pay for their tuition will only deter many from pursuing the dream of higher education.'

NUS is in favour of a new system of student financial support repayable through an income-contingent contribution from graduates, to ease the immediate problems of student hardship and the difficulties facing new graduates struggling to cope with the rigid repayments of the Student Loan Company.

NUS is totally opposed to the introduction of tuition fees. The introduction of fees would be the end of the principle of free state tuition. It will be the reintroduction of the binary divide in higher education, with cheap bargain basement universities offering cut-price education, and Ivy League colleges and courses charging as much as they can get away with.

Introducing fees would not solve the universities' cash crisis. It will definitely deter potential students from entering higher education, and it goes against the policy commitment of all the main political parties.

Students: beware banks bearing gifts

Free railcards and CDs are being used to lure new customers. But basic services are more important, writes Debbie Hill

You are more likely to get divorced than change your bank account. So if you are starting your first year of university in the next couple of months expect the banks to fight for your custom. They know you will probably stay with them for life.

Competition is fierce in the high street as banks try to dazzle new customers with free gifts – discounts, cash, cinema vouchers and CD tokens – in a bid to persuade you to open their student account.

One aspect of a student package which may attract you is the free-gift incentive. Current free offers include railcards, cinema vouchers, compact discs and videos.

But be warned: these little gifts often belie the fact that little else distinguishes one student bank account from any other – with the possible exception of free overdrafts. Students should concentrate on a bank's long-term promises, such as overdraft and loan facilities, standards of service and future benefits, not on whether they offer a cinema voucher.

But the culture of instant gratification seems to have infected the student body. So many gifts are on offer that students tend to expect some sort of incentive to open an account. In response, banks are falling over themselves to satisfy the students' demands (it is not unknown for students to open several accounts to enjoy the gifts).

Many banks are increasing the value of their gifts. In 1993 Barclays offered a £10 record voucher for anybody opening its student account. This year's new customers will receive £25 in cash and a £10 cinema voucher. And if you qualify for a credit card you receive a further £25.

NatWest has also increased its cash gift from £20 a year ago to £35 this term.

Even banks that have been reluctant to lure new customers with such incentives are succumbing to the pressure. Royal Bank of Scotland is offering a series of incentives for the first time. These include 10% off holidays and travel at home and abroad and a 20% discount on travel insurance. The bank also promises a 10% discount on 'top-selling' CDs, videos and tapes.

Jayne Goodwin, of the Royal Bank of Scotland, says: 'We have tended not to offer freebies in the past because we want to make the overall account bang on for students. But we felt the need to offer this

Massive UK demonstrations prove public anger over tuition fees threat

Students across the country will be joined by schoolchildren, parents, potential students and the general public on Saturday 1 November for demonstrations in cities throughout the United Kingdom.

Government plans to introduce fees of £1,000 per year will come into force this September if the legislation is passed by parliament.

NUS is utterly and without question opposed to tuition fees and will fight on.

The National Day of Demonstrations against tuition fees on November 1st will be the biggest show of student anger seen for many, many years. We will continue to fight for all those facing the threat of fees, as we did successfully for 20,000 gap-year students this summer. Parents, schoolchildren, would-be students and the general public feel very strongly that introduction fees would be a disaster for many who dream of the opportunity of higher education. The strength of their feeling will be seen on Saturday 1 November in the streets of the cities of the United Kingdom. We want to get the message home to each and every constituency MP that the students, would-be students and parents are against the introduction of fees.

Fees may be the universities' solution to education funding but they are hated by students and potential students and the strength of this feeling will be reflected in all our work throughout this campaign. We will oppose fees until the bitter end and have no intention of giving up, not now or in the future.

Business and industry benefit from our world-class higher education system, with top-notch graduate recruits and first-rate research and we believe they should pay more towards the cost. The business contribution is voluntary while would-be students will be forced to pay fees or abandon hope of higher education.

travel discount because students are very mobile and tend to travel quite a bit.'

The bank is also offering discounts on 'personal possession insurance' even though 'students tend to have digs in undesirable areas'.

But some banks refuse to offer any incentives to attract new customers. Chris Sonne, spokesman for the Halifax, says: 'We do not feel the need to offer free gifts because we feel our account sells itself with the other facilities we offer. We have found that students appreciate the gifts in the short term but it was the overdraft facilities and fee-free credit card that appealed in the long-term.' The Halifax offers an interest-free overdraft of up to £1,000 for up to six years, including one year after graduation.

Laura Hedgecox, 19, is starting a nursing course at Kingston University next month and had opted for a student account with Midland Bank.

Although she was attracted by the free gift of a four-year Young Person's Railcard she says she chose the Midland because of the interest-free overdraft facility of £750 in the first year, steadily rising to £1,250 in the third.

She is moving from her family home in Stockport, Greater Manchester, and will use the overdraft to cope with the added expense of living in London.

'With a bursary of £5,230 a year, after I have paid my rent of £50 a week, I will be left with just £40 for food, clothes and other expenses,' says Hedgecox.

'I want to put off taking out a student loan until the second year so until then I need a substantial overdraft to cope.'

She says the railcard appealed to her as she will be travelling home and around the country at weekends.

Christine Ross, director of financial planning at Abbey National Independent Financial Advisers, says it is essential to look beyond the free record tokens and cinema vouchers and check out which bank will serve you best in the longrun.

'Don't be swayed by these gifts offered by the banks. You must check what monetary value the account offers you on a pound-for-pound basis,' she says.

Ross says one of the most important aspects of the account is the interest-free overdraft facility. These have been increased by banks over the past few years to cope with students' deepening debt. The amount offered will vary between banks but before heading for the highest overdraft facility it is worth remembering that at some stage you are going to have to pay it off.

Barclays now promises the largest overdraft facility of £1,100 to £1,800. But the interest-free facility will be cut to just £100 in the December after your graduation. Your debt may then be transferred to a loan. Banks that have kept fee-free overdrafts to a minimum include TSB which offered £500 in the first year, increasing to £700 in the third, and Clydesdale bank with a maximum of £500.

You are likely to get some form of credit card when you open your student account so check how much you will be charged if you slip over your authorised overdraft limit.

The highest overdraft rate charged is by the Clydesdale Bank, with 33.5%, plus a fee of £12 per month. The Co-Operative Bank charges 32.92% and the Royal Bank of Scotland up to 29.8%, but this is up to your bank manager's discretion. NatWest is the only bank that will not penalise you if you go over your authorised limit. It charges an interest rate of 9.3% for authorised and non-authorised overdrafts.

The minority of you who will stay in credit should check out the interest rates offered because they vary considerably from bank to bank.

If you stay in credit with Lloyds Bank you will be given interest of 1% but if you opted foe an account with the Bank of Scotland you would receive 4.5%.

But Ross says: 'Don't just look at the charges and facilities for the years you are at university. It is important to check the charges you will face after you graduate because it will be difficult to change banks. Not many banks will want to take on an overdraft of thousands of pounds.'

The student account will end between six and 12 months after your graduation, depending on whose account you choose, so it is worth checking if your bank offers a graduate account. It should take into account the added expenses you will incur – such as the new clothes you will need for attending job interviews.

One in three students miss lectures to work part-time

NUS/GMB publish new survey on students at work

A new report into student employment published today has revealed that one in five students has failed to submit study assignments because of work and one in three students is missing lectures to work part-time. Over 78% of students working during term time say their study has been affected.

The survey, which was commissioned jointly by NUS and the GMB, found that students are working for very low wages. Over 12% are working for less than £3 an hour.

Jim Murphy, NUS President, said: 'This report is the first of its kind to look at student employment and the results make distressing reading. Record levels of hardship are now forcing the nation's students to sacrifice study to take on paid employment just to make ends meet. Students are forced to skip lectures and miss essay deadlines to spend more and more time working in pubs, burger bars, shops and factories. If they don't take on paid jobs in term time and during vacations, many students simply cannot afford to stay at college. Each statistic is a real life story of student hardship. This report is an exposé of the lengths to which some students have to go to survive. Students are being used as a cheap pool of labour forced to work in bad conditions by unscrupulous employers.

'Over half of the students surveyed were working during term time and vacations just to pay rent, living and study costs. Three out of four students say their study has been affected because of having to take paid employment during term time, and one in three misses lectures to work. The new Dearing Inquiry into higher education will look at student support and this new report into students at work will put forward compelling evidence of student hardship and all its effects on students' education opportunities today. The evidence in this report explodes the myth that students live a comfortable and cosy existence.'

Students at work survey

A recent survey by the Labour Research Department, the GMB union and NUS into the economic conditions of students in employment showed that:

- Three-quarters of students are working for less than £4 an hour and around 13% of these have pay rates of £3 an hour or less.
- Four out of ten students are employed during their term times and over two-thirds of these work through their vacations as well.
- Students most commonly work in retail and hotels/pubs/catering – industries characterised by low pay, casualisation and low levels of trade union organisation.
- Many students are working long, unsocial hours and are often not paid overtime or premium rates for doing so. The average overtime rate for a term-time worker is less than £1 more than the average hourly rate.
- Over three-quarters of students working in term time are employed for 12.5-20 hours a week. Three out of ten are working 8-12 hours a week.
- Over 80% of students working in term time get no sick pay or holiday pay and around 40% get no meal breaks or tea breaks.
- A fifth of all students reported health and safety problems in their workplaces, with the most common accidents being burns and cuts.
- 20% of students reported trade unions present in their workplaces but of the 185 who could have joined just 24 (15.5%) did so.
- A third of students reported being badly treated by their employers.
- The majority of students are working to pay for their basic living and study costs and to pay off or reduce debts.
- Over a third of all students said their employment had affected their studies but this increased to two-thirds for the students who were working during term time.
- Over 10% of all students had missed lectures or failed to submit work because of their employment. For term-time workers the proportions rose to over 30% missing lectures and 20% failing to submit work due to their employment.

ADDITIONAL RESOURCES

You might like to contact the following organisations for further information. Due to the increasing cost of postage, many organisations cannot respond to enquiries unless they receive a stamped, addressed envelope.

Association of Teachers and Lecturers
7 Northumberland Street
London, WC2N 5DA
Tel: 0171 930 6441
Fax: 0171 782 0070

Basic Skills Agency
7th Floor
Commonwealth House
1-19 New Oxford Street
London, WC1A 1NU
Tel: 0171 405 4017
Fax: 0171 404 5038
The Basic Skills Agency is the national agency for literacy, numeracy and ESOL in England and Wales. They publish a wide range of basic skills publications including books, readers, teaching packs, videos, reports, leaflets and posters.

British Accreditation Council for Independent FE and Higher Education (BAC)
Suite 401
27 Marylebone Road
London, NW1 5JS
Tel: 0171 487 4643
Fax: 0171 486 4253
Works to improve and enhance the standards of independent, further and higher education by establishing a system of accreditation.

Business and Technology Education Council (BTEC)
Central House
Upper Woburn Place
London, WC1H 0HH
Tel: 0171 413 8400
Fax: 0171 387 6068
Works to advance and promote the quality and availability of work-related education for all people in, or preparing for, employment. Produces publications.

Campaign for State Education (CASE)
158 Durham Road
London, SW20 0DG
Tel: 0181 944 8206
Fax: 0181 944 8206
Campaigns for the right of all to experience the highest quality of state education regardless of race, gender, home circumstances, ability or disability. Produces publications.

Educational Centres Association Fareham Adult Education Centre
Wickham Road
Fareham
Hants, PO16 7DA
Tel: 01329 315753
Fax: 01329 826915
Works to unite for their mutual benefit all those centres in the UK which provide adult education and which seek to promote a corporate life within a suitably equipped premises while providing opportunities for all their members to participate effectively in the activity of the centre at all levels. Produces publications.

National Association of Schoolmasters / Union of Women Teachers (NASUWT)
2 King Street
Covent Garden
London, WC2E 8HN
Tel: 0171 379 9499
Fax: 0171 497 8262

National Council for Vocational Qualifications (NCVQ)
222 Euston Road
London, NW1 2BZ
Tel: 0171 387 9898
Fax: 0171 387 0978

National Foundation for Educational Research in England and Wales (NFER)
The Mere
Upton Park
Slough, SL1 2DQ
Tel: 01753 574123
Fax: 01753 691632
Conducts research into all matters affecting education and publishes reports of the results; collects and provides information and organises conferences on educational issues.

National Union of Students (NUS)
461 Holloway Road
London, N7 6LJ
Tel: 0171 272 8900
Fax: 0171 263 5713
Represents the students of the UK locally, nationally and internationally and promotes students' interests.

NIACE – The National Institute of Adult Continuing Education
21 de Montfort Street
Leicester, LE1 7GE
Tel: 0116 255 1451
Fax: 0116 285 4514
Promotes the study and general advancement of adult continuing education.

Nuffield Foundation
28 Bedford Square
London, WC1B 3EG
Tel: 0171 631 0566
Works to achieve the advancement of education and social well-being through support for experimental or developmental work and through research.

School Curriculum & Assessment Authority (SCAA)
Newcombe House
45 Notting Hill Gate
London, W11 3JB
Tel: 0171 229 1234
Fax: 0171 243 0542

INDEX

ACKNOWLEDGEMENTS

The publisher is grateful for permission to reproduce the following material.

While every care has been taken to trace and acknowledge copyright, the publisher tenders its apology for any accidental infringement or where copyright has proved untraceable. The publisher would be pleased to come to a suitable arrangement in any such case with the rightful owner.

Chapter One: Declining Standards?

UK lags on education, © The Guardian, October 1996, *Educational competitiveness*, © International Institute for Development, *Why the English are bad at maths*, © The Independent, July 1997, *Maths: England v the rest*, © NFER, *International numeracy survey*, © Reproduced with kind permission from the Basic Skills Agency, *The myth of educational golden days*, © The Independent, August 1997, *Officials admit: it is easier to pass exams*, © Telegraph Group Limited, London 1997, *Exams that create an underclass*, © The Guardian, August 1997, *Results reveal big gulf in standards*, © Times Newspapers Limited, August 1997, *School standards conflict*, © The Guardian, December 1996, *Boys trail behind girls as pupils improve in tests*, © Telegraph Group Limited, London 1997, *Girls and boys reaching required standards*, © Telegraph Group Limited, London 1997, *Girls beat the language trap*, © The Daily Mail, September 1997, *Girls getting ahead*, © Ofsted/SCAA, *Top examiner says 'easy grade' system is undermining A-level*, © Times Newspapers Limited, August 1997, *Inspectors sent to the bottom of the class*, © The Independent, August 1997, *Parents to get schools hotline*, © The Guardian, September 1997, *Schools show progress as more pupils make grade*, © The Independent, September 1997, *Better literacy may not benefit the economy*, © The Independent, September 1997, *Poverty row looms over literacy drive*, © The Guardian, October 1997, *Older and younger*, © Reproduced with kind permission from the Basic Skills Agency, January 1995, *Basic skills projects get £32m boost*, © The Guardian, September 1997, *One in five adults on bottom rung of literacy*, © The Guardian, September 1997, *Where it all goes wrong*, © Telegraph Group Limited, London 1997, *How different countries teach maths*, © The International Mathematics and Science Society, *British pupils lead world in computer access*, © The Guardian, September 1997, *Literacy of Britons lagging far behind industrial rivals*, © Telegraph Group Limited, London 1997, *Basic Skills Programmes for Adults 1994-95*, © Reproduced with kind permission from the Basic Skills Agency, *Pupils sink in world maths league*, © The Guardian, June 1997, *'Improved' results in maths are challenged*, © Telegraph Group Limited, London 1997, *Righting reading*, © Times Newspapers Limited, June 1997, *Labour turns its back on years of 'trendy' teaching*, © Evening Standard, July 1997, *Chicago gets tough with its dunces*, © The Independent, August 1997.

Chapter Two: The Cost of an Education

Dearing decides on 'least bad plan' for tuition fees, © The Guardian, July 1997, *Sixth-formers forced to pay to study for A-levels*, © The Independent, October 1997, *Managing on a shoestring*, © The Independent, August 1997, *Student finances*, © High Fliers Research, *Higher Education student numbers*, © DfEE Statistics, *How to top up the grant*, © UCAS, Summer 1997, *The first week*, © UCAS, Summer 1997, *Tuition fees*, © Student Loans Company, *Making it stretch*, © UCAS, Summer 1997, *Ready to foot the bill?*, © The Independent, August 1997, *Student hardship affects families too*, © National Union of Students (NUS), *Annual expenditure*, © National Union of Students (NUS), *Student hardship hits record high*, © National Union of Students (NUS), *Students: beware banks bearing gifts*, © Times Newspapers Limited, August 1997, *Massive UK demonstrations prove public anger over tuition fees threat*, © National Union of Students (NUS), *One in three students miss lectures to work part-time*, © National Union of Students (NUS), *Students at work survey*, © National Union of Students (NUS).

Photographs and illustrations

Pages 4, 18, 24, 30: Andrew Smith, pages 9, 14, 17, 23, 27, 32, 39: Ken Pyne, pages 12, 21, 35, 37: Michaela Bloomfield

Craig Donnellan
Cambridge
January, 1998